Potomac Valley Watercolorists

Celebrating 40 Years 1974 – 2014

Potomac Valley Watercolorists

CELEBRATING 40 YEARS 1974 – 2014

Published by Potomac Valley Watercolorists, Inc.

Potomac Valley Watercolorists, Inc. is a 501(c)(3) non-profit juried organization of watermedia artists in the greater metropolitan Washington, DC area, established in 1974 to bring together the best watercolorists in the Potomac Valley area, to promote the development of professional quality works of art in a variety of aqueous media, to enrich the art experience and education of its members, and to make creative contributions to the community.

Book design by Stansbury Creative Services, Burke, Virginia

Printed in the United States of America by Concept Marketing, Inc., Chantilly, Virginia

Front cover: Detail from *Rose Backlit III* by Rachel Collins

Foreword

Much can change in four decades. Forty years ago, a computer took up an entire room, and a slide rule was required for higher math. Now we hold computers in our hands, and even the most advanced calculus student would be flummoxed by a slide rule. And yet, in some respects, we've made little progress. A quick peek at the Internet (an option that was not available 40 years ago), reveals that in 1974, the world was in a global economic crisis, famine in Africa was alarming, and carmakers were searching for ways to make more fuel-efficient cars in the face of energy shortages. A glance at today's news reveals that not much has changed on these fronts.

But 40 years ago, a small group of intrepid artists decided to band together to promote the art of watercolor, to provide opportunities for learning, encouragement, and exhibition that were not available to them from any other source. Potomac Valley Watercolorists has changed tremendously over the past 40 years—and yet, in some respects, is much the same as it was in the beginning.

It has changed in size, growing from a handful to now more than 200 members. It has developed an ever-widening array of programs and exhibits for members to participate in. Members now use materials that were unavailable in 1974. No one had ever heard of Yupo paper or quinacridone colors back then; now, some of our best works use those supplies.

Yet the most important aspects of this organization have remained intact over the years. PVW has always cultivated excellence, whether in members' individual paintings, the professionalism of its exhibits, or the quality of its programming. More significantly, PVW has fostered a culture of collaboration, mutual respect, and friendship among its members that uniquely benefits the artists.

The painters of PVW are a diverse group, representing a wide and varied range: we are young and not-so-young, we are of different races and creeds, we cross the political spectrum from brightest red to deepest blue, with every shade of purple in between. Our membership includes painters who make livings as lawyers, lobbyists, designers, engineers, homemakers, teachers—and even artists. Yet we all have at least one quality in common: our passion to paint has led us to seek membership in this highly regarded group.

PVW is not for the dabbler. Members are chosen once a year, in a closed jurying process. Applicants must have been accepted into at least three juried art shows in the two years prior to applying, a prerequisite that demonstrates the commitment of the painter as well as the quality of his or her art.

Still, even in our art-making, we differ. Some have never known a time when they were not making art; others discovered art later in life after completing a first career. For some, creating art is a healing action, a balm to soul in crisis. Some pick up a brush and start a painting with the ease of settling into a comfortable chair. Others struggle to push past obstacles both mental and physical to begin the painting process.

Yet amid all this diversity of background and personality, PVW members are united in facing the same challenge: how to express our unique inner vision so that others may see it. How to express it in paint.

We paint because we know that no one else can do it for us. Only we can create the art that is unique to our vision. Somewhere in the past lie piles of laundry unwashed, meals rushed or inadequate, volunteer opportunities politely ignored, bestsellers unread, closets unorganized. Someone else can take care of those matters. The important thing is to paint.

PVW provides its members with tremendous opportunity. Opportunity for a painter who is at home with small children to exhibit work in a professional setting—and sell it. Opportunity for a painter who delves deeply into law on a daily basis to take a week off and be challenged with a demanding workshop, trying new techniques and materials. Opportunity for a painter who stares at a computer screen all week to travel with other painters and contemplate works of art instead.

Yet most PVW members, if asked what the most important aspect of membership in this organization is, would answer simply: the people. As we each strive to paint, in our individual way, we share a deep bond. We understand one another's challenges, frustrations, heartbreaks, and triumphs in ways few others can. A solidarity, a companionship has developed that is a hallmark of this organization. We help each other grow in our shared passion. We invest time and energy to maintain PVW as a vital place of learning and development for one another.

Forty years strong, PVW remains a vibrant force in the mid-Atlantic art scene. Through the pages of this book, the spirit of PVW and its diverse membership—each individual vision—shines forth.

—Carolyn Marshall Wright, on behalf of all presidents, current and past, who remain enthusiastic members of the Potomac Valley Watercolorists:

Carolyn Grossé Gawarecki	Gwendolyn C. Bragg
Judy Wengrovitz	Jane Cordes Simanis
Margaret Graham Kranking	Gloria Logan
Frank H. Spink	Rachel B. Collins
Betsy LeBleu Curry	Sally H. Olson
Pauline Davis Lorfano	Christine Lashley
Yolanda Frederikse	Peter B. Ulrich
Chica Brunsvold	Carolyn Marshall Wright
Christine A. Heyse	Catherine Hillis

PVW – An Informal History

Like so many things, Potomac Valley Watercolorists was created to fill a need.

Watercolorist Carolyn Grossé Gawarecki was living in Northern Virginia in the early 1970s and, she says, "It was an exciting time for me. I was actively teaching and painting watercolor, so I joined all the local art groups." But only one, the Washington Watercolor Association, was devoted solely to water media, and Carolyn found it difficult to get to meetings in the District of Columbia.

The solution? Start a new watercolor society. Carolyn asked several of her students to join her, and seven founding members – Carolyn, Faye Owens, Carolyn Richardson, Nancy Erickson, Carl Barnes, Allen Mays, and Helen Dilley Barsalou – held a series of planning meetings at Carolyn's home.

PVW had its first official meeting at the Thomas Jefferson Library in Falls Church, Virginia, on April 8, 1974. Dues for the first year were $5, and in a few months, the group had 35 charter members. (Seven are members to this day: Carolyn Gawarecki, Helen Barsalou, Judy Wengrovitz, Chica Brunsvold, Marge Alderson, Margaret Kranking, and Marjean Willett.)

The group wanted to represent the highest levels of artistry, so began requiring that new members be juried in, asking outside professional artists to serve as jurors.

The fledgling society defined watercolor as "any aqueous medium framed under glass" and included transparent watercolor, gouache, casein, and acrylic. Meetings were sporadic, but PVW occasionally invited speakers to discuss aspects of water media, and members painted with one another on a casual basis.

"We didn't have a lot of formal programs, because we didn't want to do all that work," recalls Carolyn. "We all wanted to paint, not tie ourselves down with a lot of organizational duties."

As PVW grew, however, so did the number of people willing to do just that – pitch in and help develop programs, workshops, exhibits, trips, and other activities. Today the organization has 220 members from within the Potomac Valley region and beyond.

PVW brings in nationally known artists to lead a wide variety of workshops and mounts several exhibits each year, including a popular weekend show and sale each fall. PVW membership has become synonymous with a high standard of skill, creativity, and commitment to water media. The organization enjoys a regional – even national – reputation for excellence, both for the artistic mastery of its members and for their dedication to this thriving group of painters who take their art, but not themselves, very seriously.

– Deborah Conn

Acknowledgements

Bringing an anniversary collection such as this to the light of day requires the wholehearted effort of many, many individuals. The first thanks should go to all the artists who are represented by the beautiful images in this book, for being such amazing painters and doing their best to provide all the pieces necessary for publication.

President Carolyn Marshall Wright and the PVW Board serving from March 2011 to April 2013 have given unwavering support and guidance to this project, for which the whole organization owes a huge thanks.

After several preliminary surveys and discussions at PVW membership meetings in 2011 and 2012, the real work on the book started with a meeting in June 2012, attended by Sally Olson, Florence Setzer, Sarah Andrews, and Judy and Sy Wengrovitz.

Other volunteers came forward to help out in the early days, most notably Jill Poyerd, who developed and managed the database of participants throughout the project.

Thanks are due to photographer Greg Staley, who offered several photo shoots to give all artists the opportunity to have professional images of their work. The photo shoots were managed and hosted by PVW volunteers Sheldon Ruben, Jane Simanis, Tricia DeWeese, Marilyn Milici, and Carolyn Wright.

A huge amount of work was done by the four people who joined me in receiving the images and texts from the artists, as this involved much close examination of the entries and communication with all the artists: Jackie Dinora, Pat Porter, Jill Poyerd, and Florence Setzer.

The jury process was managed by Pat Porter, who devised a computer-based system for the presentation of images to the jurors and for the documentation of their choices. She was assisted by Sally Olson, who served as scribe for the jurying. Many thanks are also due to the jurors, who prefer to remain anonymous.

Once the images for the book were chosen, five editors worked with the artist texts to bring some standardization in style and format, while retaining the flavor of the individual artists' words: Sarah Andrews, Howard Cincotta, Debby Conn, Florence Setzer, and Harriet Westfall.

Special thanks are also due to Carolyn Wright for composing the Foreword on behalf of all presidents of PVW, past and current; to Debby Conn for assembling and writing the history of our organization; to Jean Gill, Tony Neville, and Sally Olson for researching and putting together the In Memoriam list; and to Francesca Creo for working on the list of current members and their recognition in the world of watermedia beyond our Washington metro area.

Although the essence of our book is due to the painting images of our artists, the beautiful presentation and layout are due to our designer, Valerie Stansbury, who has been wonderfully patient, understanding and helpful from the very first days of her involvement in the project. We consider ourselves fortunate to have had the opportunity to work with her.

Warmest thanks are also due to Jean Gill, Tricia DeWeese, Susan Herron, and Gloria Logan for additional special support, to Debby Conn and Howard Cincotta for their final review of the texts, to Alice Kale and Charlotte Landis for organizing the distribution of this book, and to the PVW members who have volunteered to house the books and help with the distribution.

Everyone mentioned, and others as well, have given heart and soul to this project, knowing that we want to give appropriate recognition to the organization that has given us so much, both personally and professionally. For this, all of us are profoundly grateful.

— Rachel Collins
For the entire PVW Book Team

Our Most Heartfelt Thanks Go to

Rachel Collins, without whom this book would not have been produced. It was Rachel who had the initial vision for it, far enough in advance of PVW's 40th year to honor that anniversary. Rachel's ideas encompassed not only the final product but all the myriad minute details needed for its completion. Her enthusiasm was contagious, leading to the great level of cooperation and collaboration outlined in the preceding paragraphs. We, the members of PVW, recognize that it is in great part due to Rachel – her persistence and energy, her thoroughness and creativity – that this book exists, and we are profoundly grateful.

— Carolyn Marshall Wright
For the Potomac Valley Watercolorists

The Paintings

Gretchen Thompson

gretchenthepainter@gmail.com

On a beautiful day in May I attended the graduation of a dear friend's daughter. The ceremony was held at the National Institutes of Health in a building that was once a cloister. This beautiful window was in that building. The shapes of the window, enhanced by the bright sunlight, were an awesome sight. I was fortunate to have my camera to capture the moment. I knew then that I needed to paint this beautiful window.

Inner Sanctum
watercolor, 15 x 9

Duet

watercolor, 13 x 20

This painting was the first of a series of watercolors delving into the captivating lives of horses. The faces of horses can be so full of expression, their communications intense and complex. On this crisp fall day, Fernando casts his attentive eye on Stella, the mare. These two friends approach each other with gentleness, their interest in one another so plain to see. I created the textures of their furry coats and manes with layers of transparent brushwork, lifting, and resist.

Mak Dehejia

301-938-9144
mdehejia@gmail.com
dehejiaart.com

This transparent watercolor is one of a series of works painted to record my unforgettable experience spending four days in the home of the celebrated English watercolorist Ron Ranson. I was amazed at the variety of detail that Ron could coax out of his wide hake brush. He patiently taught me the intricacies of using this brush to paint a variety of strokes, using it either full-face or tweaking a corner to make finer marks and so on. This painting was made using the Ranson hake, an 04 rigger, and fingernails for scratching out tree trunks and grasses! The colors used were raw sienna, permanent alizarin crimson, Payne's grey for the sky, and burnt umber with a touch of French ultramarine for the tree. This picture was juried into shows at the Art League of Alexandria as well as the Yellow Barn at Glen Echo.

Lone Oak

watercolor, 11 x 15

Tricia DeWeese

triciadeweese@verizon.net

I could only imagine this gentleman's story. I was drawn to his demeanor and a sense of reflection on his past. Was he a jazz musician, an actor, an artist? His violet hat and plume, along with his silky white suit and black shirt, announced his style. I wanted to capture the mystery of where he has been and where he is heading, literally and allegorically, with a pensive atmosphere.

Having worked with a triad of Winsor red, Winsor blue (red shade), and Winsor yellow for the past 15 years or more, I exchanged my Winsor red for permanent rose to achieve a stronger violet without compromising the intensity of my palette.

New Orleans Character
watercolor, 30 x 22

Roberta Day

7531 Woodberry Lane
Falls Church, Virginia 22042
703-560-5528
rdaymell@msn.com

One August day, the sunlight on this clump of tall grass in a garden park caught my startled attention. I had seen it on other days, and the leaves were unremarkable shades of brown. But on this occasion, sections of the leaves were a rainbow of colors and called out to my camera and paintbrush. I used a digital photo-editing program to enhance the colors even further, transferred a drawing made from the photograph to a sheet of Arches cold press, 140 lb. watercolor paper, and, with continued excitement and engagement, executed the painting in a direct manner.

Garden Surprise

watercolor, 22 x 30

Deborah Conn

debconn@cox.net

deborahconn.com

This painting is one of a series that uses both watercolor and hand-painted papers to explore figures. I have always been drawn to portraits and the human form, and I've found that adding collage has allowed me to be more expressive and less tied to my source material. I enjoy the perspective of this figure and her expansive, relaxed posture.

Feet First
watercolor and collage, 15x 13

Roberta P. Lintner

7925 Ellet Road
Springfield, Virginia 22151
703-321-8826

The sunlight streaming through the branches of the pine forest creates myriad patterns of light and dark on the palmetto plants. Their endless variety is a source of inspiration for me. In October the rich greens and golds of these tropical plants are at their peak on Hatteras Island. These intense colors were the foundation of my painting.

I started painting the foreground palm fronds first, trying to make an interesting interplay of shapes and cast shadows. I then put in the background shapes in more subdued colors. The result was *October Palmettos.*

October Palmettos

watercolor, 38 x 30

Margaret M. Suddeth

Her Brother's Embrace

transparent watercolor, 17 x 25

Portraits can have an emotional connection to the viewer that other types of paintings don't have. I strive to create this connection in every one of my portraits. I want to capture more than a subject's likeness; I want you to feel that you have discovered something special about the subject – a bit of his true and inner beauty. I consider myself fortunate to have captured the moment portrayed in this painting of a brother and his young sister.

I was photographing them with their brother for a group portrait when Nick bent down to embrace Caroline. He was leaving the next day to join the Navy. I like to think this painting glows in many ways – the way the sun lights the faces, the emotions expressed by the subjects, and the luminous qualities of the transparent watercolor used to paint the image.

Helen Dilley Barsalou

7106 Cynthia Court
Annandale, Virginia 22003
703-560-3977
dilleyarts@cox.net
helendilleybarsalou.com

River Rapids

watercolor, 21 x 28

River Rapids is part of a series I created from listening to *The Moldau River,* by Smetana. His music begins with light tinkling notes as a small stream starts in the mountains. I started with a painting of this. The music grows as the stream is joined by a second one to form the Moldau River. My imagination created paintings of these at a number of different stages. The music then describes a fox hunt and village dancers. At one point the river goes through some rocky rapids, and the music becomes more active and exciting. That was my inspiration for this painting.

I went on to paint other phases with a more majestic tone as the river widens and flows past Prague and an ancient fortress. It finally winds through the lowlands on its way to the sea, and the music becomes more expansive and powerful. I have been on this beautiful river. No, I did not see all of these stages described by the music – except in my imagination.

Trudy Levy

trudy@trudylevy.com

For this painting I used handmade papers from a sampler. The papers were tub-sized hot press, cold press, and rough surfaces in both white and subtle colors. I had never used watercolor on tinted paper and it became both an experiment and a learning experience. When I found a bird's nest on my lawn, I thought it would be an appropriate subject to try with the beige cold press sample. I found some acorns to add to the composition. Because the paper was tinted, I had to use some white gouache for the highlights. The paper color is so lovely that I decided that I did not need to add a background.

Nest and Pinecones
watercolor with gouache highlights, 7 x 5

Carolyn
Marshall Wright

1841 MacArthur Drive
McLean, Virginia 22101
703-534-2798
c.marshall.wright@gmail.com

Our family has a tradition of hiking in Riverbend Park, Virginia, each spring to see the bluebells. The pathway runs along the edge of the Potomac River, and if you time it right, the bluebells run rampant! In the title, I've deliberately played with the word, trying to evoke coy southern belles in hoop skirts at the ball, as these flowers conjure that image for me. I've tried a number of times to capture their fragile luminosity in a painting; this one comes closest so far. I used peacock blue, permanent rose, and new gamboge over an underpainting. To create the underpainting, I took the paper to the beach in Duck, North Carolina, where I held the paper under the waves to let the sand wash over it. Once I had an interesting pattern of sand on the paper, I carefully took it away from the water's edge and immediately dropped color onto it. The pigments oozed and swirled around the edges of the sand. Once dry, the sand was removed. The random, organic forms created by this technique provided a fitting foundation for the composition of this painting.

The Belles of Riverbend Park
transparent watercolor, 7 x 5

Sycamore, Moonglow

watercolor with iridescent medium, 29 x 41

Margaret Huddy

703-356-2363
703-477-5829 cell
mthuddy@gmail.com
huddy.com

I found my muse in 1985 when we moved to McLean, Virginia. There, just a few blocks from my house, lives a magnificent, historic sycamore tree that is as old as our country. Because it is nearby, I have literally photographed it from sunrise to moonrise – but only in winter. Those photographs have inspired the creation of 43 paintings of the same tree. The white bark reflects light so beautifully and allows me to have fun with the color.

I do not use masking fluid but paint the sky between each branch, usually starting around the central trunk and matching the color in the sky holes as I spread out from the trunk. I use several graded glazes in the sky. When that is finished, I paint the tree and the main branches, then the twigs. The background trees, which help to give it a sense of scale, I paint last.

I work in a limited palette of reds, blues, and yellows, always thinking of dark against light and warm against cool. The paper is 555 lb. Arches cold press. At the end, I washed a glaze of iridescent medium over the moon and on the branches that face it.

Barry D. Lindley

3131 Connecticut Avenue, NW
Apt 2904
Washington, DC 20008
202-621-9013
lindleybd@gmail.com
BarryLindleyArt.com

Morning at the Marina

transparent watercolor, 15 x 22

My art reflects delight in the sensuous qualities of paint on paper as expressed through abstract design. In this painting I strove to share my connection with the boats at rest as the low, rosy morning sun rolled back the mist. Free forms of rich, mingling watercolor are countered by a more detailed rendering of the boats. The verticals of the masts create energy and expectation as well as interlocking the shapes.

I began with drawings and did a quick, *plein air* acrylic painting on canvas panel on site at Belle Haven Marina near Alexandria, Virginia. Using the panel plus my photos and sketches, I finished painting in my studio. In style, my paintings are largely interpretive or expressive realism. I choose medium, character of brush work, compositional emphasis, and color relationships to represent how I look at the subject, how I feel about it, and what I want you to experience.

Joan Lok

P.O. Box 6271
Columbia, Maryland 21045
410-730-7597
joanlok128@gmail.com
joanlok.com

I wanted to create contrast between the delicate waterfall and the massive rock texture in *Emerald Fall*. After deciding the general composition, I crinkled the rice paper to create what I call "peaks and valleys" of the paper. Without flattening the peaks and valleys, I alternately layered different shades of black, green, and brown ink on the paper. This technique creates convincing edges and shadows of rocks. After the entire piece dried, I wet it again and painted the waterfall wet on wet for the soft, fluid effect of water. I refined the overall composition with stones and pebbles along the fall.

Emerald Fall
sumi-e ink and watercolor on rice paper, 27 x 18

Sydney Morgan

919-424-7182
sydneymorgangalleries.com

My husband and I rented a casita in Santa Fe. One day, after looking at galleries in town, we returned in the afternoon to this scene in which sunlight was streaming through the window illuminating three apples I had placed in a pottery dish on our small dining table. The lighting was so dramatic and beautiful. I immediately began taking photographs, did some quick sketches, and made notes on color temperature and reflected light.

I created the painting later in my studio on 140 lb. cold press paper using multiple watercolor glazes that were allowed to dry thoroughly between layers. *Santa Fe Still* was juried into group shows and also won several awards.

Santa Fe Still
watercolor, 22 x 19

Clearing by Evening

acrylic and water-soluble sticks, 14 x 31

Betty Calabria

672 Ridge Road
Bridgewater, Virginia 22812
540-828-3120
bettycalabria@hughes.net

Barrier islands off the coast of South Carolina provide front-row seating to observe winter storms. Storms accost beaches and marshlands as grey armies from the ocean. Skies left behind are ones scrubbed clean in spectacular displays of light and color. Here, I executed the horizontal format with its linear forms in paint in response to the spectacular parades of light and color that sometimes follow a storm. I created *Clearing by Evening* with acrylic paint on primed BFK print paper.

Lorrie Herman

703-906-5815
lahermanart@cox.net
lorrieherman.com

I am fortunate that I live close to many charming historic towns. This painting is of Loudoun Street just off the main historic area in Leesburg, Virginia. The hollyhocks were in bloom, and the dark ivy in the background just made their pink color pop. Although this painting is not without summer blooms, I enjoy *plein air* painting these townscapes, especially when the landscape hasn't greened up yet. The buildings have color, structure, and lots of character. It's about capturing a sense of place and time.

I start off with my sketch using a medium mop and lay in my initial wash, leaving my whites. Then I go back and lay in some darks to establish my value range. I continue mixing the colors I need, painting in the middle tones. All of my greens and greys are mixed for the foliage and shadows. The next pass is adjusting values and then popping in some details. Done!

Loudoun Street

transparent watercolor, 12 x 15

Millie S. Shott

6705 Melville Place
Chevy Chase, Maryland 20815
301-652-1435

Winter Birch was painted on 140 lb. Saunders Waterford watercolor paper with transparent watercolors. It was painted wet on wet with the main trunk of the tree masked to preserve the white of the paper. Once the background of the painting was complete, the masking was removed from the trunk. I then completed the tree by texturizing the bark of the tree and adding small details.

Winter Birch

watercolor, 15 x 11

Alice Kale

703-683-3988
alicekaleartist@yahoo.com

In *New Life,* I've attempted to show the gradual unfolding of spring. I often paint birds' nests, this particular one being based on a discovery in our yard. Although the eggs probably belonged to a robin, I substituted those of my pet cockatiel, an ever-hopeful layer of eggs.

I love painting the complexities of branches and enjoy the challenge of using a square format.

I usually begin with a general idea, but often the process assumes a life of its own until I decide that the painting is finished.

New Life

transparent watercolor, 17 x 17

Row by Row

Deb Cohan

deborahcohan@yahoo.com

watercolor, 13 x 19

The Folklife Festival sponsored by the Smithsonian is an event I anticipate every summer. It is a wonderful place to learn about different countries, cultures, and ideas. Camera in hand, I spend hours exploring the sensory playground. The inspiration for this painting came from the visiting country of Bhutan. What drew me to this scene was both the intensity with which the weaver was working and the contrasts of color and texture the scene provided. The weaver is wearing a skirt and vest of shimmering silk, yet she is barefoot and her hair is wilting in the ever-present Washington humidity. While the frame of her loom is polished, other parts are rough slats of worn wood and broken bamboo.

I used different techniques in an attempt to heighten these contrasts. For her skirt and vest I began with a warm yellow and built the colors through glazing. I painted the weaving directly, with each color slightly muted.

Kate Niner

britrose@juno.com

High and Dry

watercolor, 13 x 22

This painting was inspired by a photograph of dinghies on the River Dart in Dartmouth, England. At low tide, the dinghies and small boats sit on the mud with buckets attached to the outboard motors to protect the propellers – a unique sight. I literally poured the mud – a technique that requires successive layers of paint (usually at least three) to be poured onto wet paper and allowed to mix, with progressive ranges of values masked between each pour once the paper is completely dry. The result in this case was a more interesting and eye-catching background that showcases the wonderful qualities of watercolor, onto which I painted the dinghies using a more traditional dry brush method.

Anne Hanna

302-732-3879
artfoxag@msn.com
annehanna.com

I photographed this whooping crane at the Patuxent Wildlife Refuge while he was eating a gift of crabs. I was hosting a group of agricultural high school Scouts from Mississippi, and we toured the facility.

Whoops
watercolor, 29 x 22

Tammy Wiedenhaefer

tammywiedenhaefer@gmail.com
tammywiedenhaefer.com

Three years ago I went on an African safari. I was thrilled to see all the animals in their natural habitat and not in a zoo. The zebras quickly became some of my favorite animals. One would think they would be easy to see, but their stripes hide them amazingly well. Because the stripes are so definitive and methodical, I decided to paint the surroundings using a loose wet-in-wet technique incorporating splattering, spraying water, blowing puddles of pigment, negative painting, and even a bit of salt. I kept the color of the stripes relatively uniform. I used the quality of the edges and the addition of warmer tones to define the depth of field. The visual harmony of nature always amazes me.

In Plain Sight
watercolor, 22 x 14

Anna M. Shuman

annashuman@comcast.net
yellowbarnstudio.com/gr/shuman/htm

Painting is a form of meditation for me, a way of focusing and quieting my mind. As I concentrate on the painting, I become aware of the exquisite beauty that surrounds us every day. My thoughts dissolve and become irrelevant; only the moment of seeing and connecting through my painting exists. I often choose a single flower, such as the one in *Bird of Paradise*, as my subject matter. Doing so allows me to experience both the flower's individual beauty and its universal perfection.

Bird of Paradise

watercolor, 22 x 30

Cindi Lewis

clewisart@comcast.net
clewisart.com

September

transparent watercolor, 7 x 10

On a September drive through the Northern Neck of Virginia, I was struck by the late summer and early autumn colors in the strong sunlight on the fields – and the contrasting shadows in the bordering trees. My objective in this image was to work as simply and quickly as possible to avoid fussiness and muddy colors. I used masking fluid to save the fence so that I could freely paint the fields in a few brushstrokes, and I dropped pure dark pigments onto a light background to create the shadows in the trees and under the bush in the foreground.

Jim Cobren

cobrenart@aol.com

This painting depicts the male-dominated tyranny of the past with modern times. I tried to show the dark of the past with the lighter, cooler side felt today, where women are no longer looked down upon but embraced. I painted the ladies on the bench to add interest and controversy.

Changing Times
watercolor, 28 x 18

Lynda D. Pitman

lyndapitman@aol.com

When I was a child my father grew prize-winning roses, and I remember our summer garden filled with their fragrance. I have quite a few rose bushes in my own garden now, but I don't have my father's touch, so I paint them much better than I grow them. My favorites to work on are these big, old-fashioned cabbage roses – the more complex the better. I paint flower petals first, backgrounds last. I paint each petal individually, and if a petal is really large I break it down into sections. I build up glazes of color working wet in wet until the values are the way I want them. A hard-edged shadow is done last without wetting the paper. Before moving on I try to make the petal as finished as I can. That doesn't mean I don't go back to these areas as the work progresses – I do. I constantly tweak "finished" areas to make sure colors and values are consistent throughout the work. I have been known to take out an entire "finished" section and re-work it. Lastly, using dark values throughout the work is so important – they make the stars shine.

Summer Bouquet
watercolor, 24 x 19

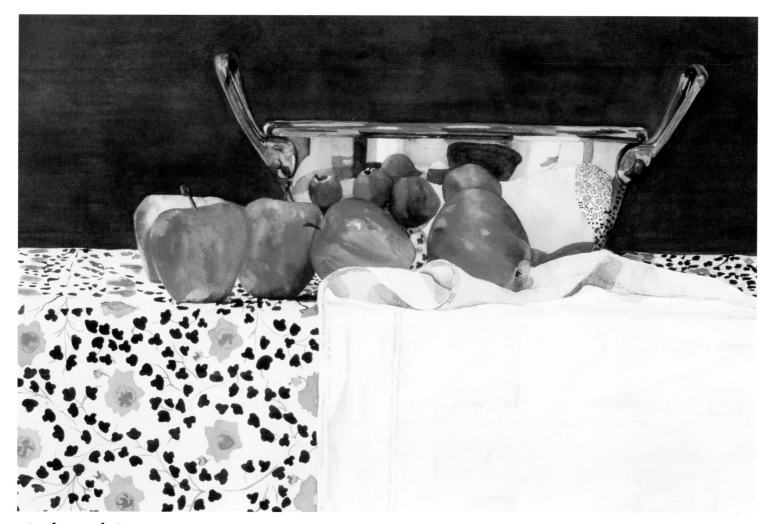

Dell Keathley

dellkeathley.com

Apples and Copper

watercolor, 14 x 19

The subject in this painting is a wonderful copper bowl that is both rich in color and highly reflective. Because I work from life, I was able to adjust the lighting to my advantage, showing the bowl's qualities by using strong value contrasts. I began by painting the apples in the foreground, allowing each layer of color to dry completely before applying the next. I then put a very light transparent wash of permanent rose and yellow over certain areas of the copper to unify all of the shapes and reflections, always letting the paint dry before continuing. When I was partially through with the apples on the table, I began to slowly paint the reflected apples. All but one of the reflected apples had very dark values, which allows the viewer to immediately distinguish between them and the foreground apples. As the painting neared completion I concentrated on all of the other rich darks being reflected. It just required looking and comparing over and over again.

Katherine Sullivan

4730 North 17th Street
Arlington, Virginia 22207
703-276-0939
katherinesullivan@verizon.net

Inspiration can come from anywhere. Most of mine comes from nature. I am lucky to have a house in the small town of Colonial Beach, Virginia. The town is a bird sanctuary and has an abundance of water-related wildlife including fish, crabs, and birds. After I had painted several images of peeler crabs, people began to call me the crab lady. Because of that, a woman I did not know brought me five leftover cooked crabs. What a lucky occurrence. Those crabs became the source of many more paintings. My first step is always to take a picture. I am not quick, and working from photographs allows me time to design. I rearranged, duplicated, and flipped the images of the crabs to create an entirely new composition. The newspaper background was a separate element. I drew out pages and columns and carefully measured type lines, which gave me flexibility in the design. I wanted to keep the focus on the crabs and not the background. I used traditional techniques, working in transparent watercolors on 300 lb. paper.

Tasty Treats

transparent watercolor, 22 x 30

Vita M. Sims

vita@vitadesigns.com
vitadesigns.com

I painted *NYC Reflections* in the studio. It is an emotional and expressive watercolor that I would call a psychological portrait. The intention was to use color, line, and shape intuitively to distort and reveal the inner and outer worlds of life and relationships. I began with a photograph taken without flash that was dark and mysterious. I initially sketched loosely with a watercolor pencil and a graphite crayon to define the figure and the interior. I then used watercolor in shades of purple, green, ochre, and rose to define and further develop my subject.

NYC Reflections
watercolor on Japanese paper, 40 x 26

Jan H. Burns

1829 Horseback Trail
Vienna, Virginia 22182
703-281-4870
janhburns@cal.berkeley.edu

In *Autumn Leaves,* red and yellow leaves caught by the wind swirl upward and then slowly descend down toward the earth before the snow encases the world.

The process I employed began simply with the words "the woods." Using this as inspiration, and with no preliminary sketches, I drew the images of the bases of trees and their twisted, gnarled root systems directly onto the paper with neutral-colored paint. Displeased with the results, I covered the root images with what was to become the first of many layers of white and off-white paint and darkened the top portion of the paper. The painting evolved into a simple high-horizon composition. I finished the piece with a series of quick, slashing marks of various colors of acrylic and watercolor paint that added excitement to the surface of the paper. On one level the painting is an abstract study of contrasting values, colors, and textures. On a different level it represents a contrast between the lively, colorful autumn leaves and the quiet, somber winter snow.

Autumn Leaves
acrylic and watercolor on paper, 24 x 19

Roslyn Perluck Latto

703-684-8073
larrylatto@comcast.net

For many years I have been a volunteer tutor at a nearby elementary school. This has been an enjoyable and rewarding job. Particularly interesting has been the change through the years from native-born kids to children from faraway places; some have very little English, yet are eager to learn the language of their adoptive country. In painting this scene, I have stressed that it takes patience and concentration on the parts of both student and teacher.

It Takes 2 To Tutor

watercolor, 13 x 16

Michele Rea

9890 Oxcrest Drive
Fairfax Station, Virginia 22039
703-495-9260
703-395-8104 cell
Michele@reaproductions.com
michelerea.com

This painting is a partial view of an old gate to the cemetery of a church in lower Manhattan. I was first drawn to the dome shape of the door set into a long brick wall around the centuries-old cemetery. I love old, architectural subjects that show their age. I cropped my subject many different ways with my camera until I arrived at this composition. I wanted to show just enough of the subject to draw the viewer in. I love the contrast of smooth bricks and rough, chipped, rusted metal on the door and hinge. I applied many layers of paint and carefully lifted off sections to create the different surfaces. I spent the most time on the rust, which is one of my favorite textures to paint.

Old Cemetery Gate

watercolor, 14 x 19

William Doying

817 Duke Street
Alexandria, Virginia 22314
703-549-8177
703-362-3611 cell
cwdoying@aol.com

I took the reference photograph for this painting at Alexandria's George Washington's Birthday Parade (Lincoln and the Civil War play a part, too). I was struck by what seemed a very natural, easy posture of the reenactor and by the handsomeness of the horse; the resulting painting gives me a lot of satisfaction. In the photograph, the background is the corner of Duke and Saint Asaph Streets in Old Town, which seemed to me to distract from the essence of the painting; nor did I want to invent some "period" setting, so I omitted it altogether. That the result doesn't conform to the "rules" for a vignette does not bother me much, and evidently did not bother its purchaser. As with others of my best paintings, transparent watercolor is the medium – but some areas, especially the body of the horse, were applied quite heavily, with some mixing on the paper.

Confederate Cavalry Reenactor
watercolor, 12 x 11

Florence Setzer

setzerf@netscape.net

These boulders lie along the Colorado River in the Grand Canyon. I was struck by the pleasing contrast between the solid shapes of the boulders and the linear strata of the rock beneath, and by the intensity of the sunlight on the rocks. I wanted to paint the subject *en plein air* but there was no shade and no escape from the desert sun. Instead I took photographs and painted the scene later in the studio. I painted the shaded cliff in wet-in-wet layers. In the foreground I used sharp edges and strong value contrast to convey the intense sunlight. I tried to capture the vivid hues and warm reflections of the red rock.

Canyon Rocks
watercolor, 20 x 14

Colleen Sabo

Friendship, Maryland
301-855-6128
301-467-9253 cell
colleensabo@comcast.net

I painted *Cloud Nine* during an early autumn visit to Maine. The craggy coastline and rocks were absolutely gorgeous, and at one point I felt like I was on "Cloud Nine" with all of the color and linear feeling of the rocks. This painting has been juried into three exhibitions in New York City: The Catharine Lorillard Wolfe Art Club in 2012, the Allied Artists of America 98th Annual Exhibit in 2011, and the Salmagundi Club's Non-Members Juried Exhibit in 2011.

Cloud Nine
watercolor, 14 x 29

Jacquelyn J. Dinora

2140 Welchpoole Court
Dunkirk, Maryland 20754
301-855-5625
jdinora@comcast.net

Orange Pekoe is one of a series of paintings using tea as a theme. I have a collection of antique sugar bowls and creamers and a small garden that supply endless ideas for new work. The subject itself offers many possibilities, as many cultures around the world have lovely ceremonies involved in the making of tea. I always get questions on creating a very dark background. I work the background first, layering orange, then black (yes, black!) in 10 to 12 layers. I protect my image area with liquid mask, press-and-seal wrap, removable contact paper, and artist's tape so I can splash and dash the background without staining the detail area of the painting. When the background is completely dry I begin to remove paint with a sponge or with an airbrush filled with water until I get the look I want. This painting won First Place in the first online gallery show of the Maryland Federation of Art and was accepted in the Baltimore Watercolor Society's 2012 Mid-Atlantic show.

Orange Pekoe

watercolor, 22 x 30

Jung Lea Smith

jung@jungsmith.com
jungsmith.com

This is a portrait of a friend's granddaughter, happily posing for the picture. I enjoy painting portraits, especially trying to catch different people's expressions. Most of my portraits are done from good photos. I also like landscapes, flowers, and other subjects, both realistic and abstract. I paint most of my work with regular watercolor on watercolor paper, although sometimes I use oil and acrylic on canvas or yupo paper and pastel on paper.

Young Girl
watercolor, 14 x 11

Harriet Westfall

703-524-4225
hwestfall41@verizon.net

We had driven to the bay for a seafood treat, and while waiting for a table I saw a worker preparing to load bushels of crabs. I was struck by the mahogany darkness of his skin, which contrasted with the white heat of the parking lot. I took a photo as surreptitiously as possible. I used pale watercolor washes to set the background and retained some whites. For the bushels I used rough strokes to capture the woody texture of the baskets.

Balancing Act
watercolor, 13 x 10

Betsy LeBleu Curry

jbcurry@verizon.net

watercolor, 15 x 22

Gravely 1928

A historic Fairfax farmhouse was scheduled for demolition when the last occupant, the widow of the farmer, died. On the way to choose a place to work on a painting of the property, I spotted this wonderful piece of rusting equipment in a sunlit open shed. I sat right down and devoted my first efforts to capturing on watercolor paper this mysterious tool. This painting "just fell off my brush." Years later at an outdoor art show in Lexington, Virginia, an aged farmer in coveralls, unconsciously chewing long sprigs of seeded grass, visited my booth. All of a sudden he stopped, took a second look at this painting, and said: "Huh! It's a 1928 Gravely!"

Natalie R. Fleming

58 Woods Edge Ct.
St. Charles, Missouri 63304
636-288-0996
n.j.fleming@att.net
framations.com

I painted the chrysanthemums from actual mums sitting on the windowsill of my studio. The flowers were lovely, but the background was not very interesting. I thought that an outdoor setting would be better, so I invented the porch and outdoors for the background. The important thing to me was the change of color on the flowers as the sun filtered through the petals.

Mums on My Porch

transparent watercolor, 25 x 29

Brenda Will Kidera

3591 Hipsley Mill Road
Woodbine, Maryland 21797
410-489-0431
brendakidera@gmail.com
KideraFineArt.com

I've done many group portraits and they always present challenges, especially when they include children. I was at my neighbor's and saw these kids playing. I asked them to sit for me and I gave them Fudgsicles to keep them occupied while I spent several minutes taking about 50 photographs. Although I made suggestions to them, they did a nice job interacting naturally. It took about a week to put together my drawing, splicing heads, arms and legs, moving and adding flower pots, simplifying the background. It didn't feel balanced--it was in need of a fifth figure. One of my cats was going to be featured, but this dog arrived with a friend one day and I took photos in my backyard from a vantage point I recollected from my initial shoot. He was reduced to a smaller dog type so he fit well in the composition. When it came to the painting process, I made further changes: Fudgsicles became colorful Popsicles, I adjusted clothing and skin tones, and I modified values.

Popsicles!
watercolor, 24 x 22

43

Connie Ward Woolard

3922 Havard Street
Silver Spring, Maryland 20906
301-946-4217

Poole's General Merchandise Store

acrylic 22 x 28

Through the years we have taken many family trips to Seneca Locks on the Potomac River and have walked along the C&O Canal enjoying the beauty of the place. Exploring a bit more while spending the day with friends, I looked again at Poole's Store and felt I was seeing it for the first time. It was a wonderful place and I had to stop and take photos. Much later I decided to paint a portrait of it, using acrylic on 300 lb. Arches watercolor paper. This painting was the result. I hope it preserves the store for posterity, which is what I want to accomplish with all my architectural portraits. I am always drawn to nostalgic subjects and try to capture my own feelings about them, whether in a landscape, house portrait, or still life. I like painting still lifes featuring family heirloom china. Painting is always a joy whatever the subject.

Mary Cannell Andrews

mca663@gmail.com

Painting a black fur subject and not letting it look flat was a challenge. I used Winsor blue, Winsor green, and permanent alizarin to mix the black, making it possible to warm it up or cool it down. It was necessary to quickly snap a photo to use as reference before rescuing my orchid!

The Orchid Connoisseur   *watercolor, 14 x 18*

Karen Norman

7 Thomas Drive
Silver Spring, Maryland 20904
301-622-3770
waterkart@gmail.com
knorman.com

The viewer sees past the protective
and nurturing plant that has sent
out a new offshoot. Below are
the bowl of pears and another
lone pear all resting on a pebbled
surface. The lone pear is not out of
sight or completely away from the
light that bathes the bowl of pears.
Instead the light beckons.

Another Dimension
watercolor, 30 x 22

JoAnne Ramsey

jaramsey@comcast.net

Painting *Jazzy Duo* was both fun and challenging. You can almost hear the brush on the drum and the plunking sound of the base. Warm colors cooled by a touch of blue suit the hot style of the jazz. Before starting the actual painting, I randomly added torn pieces of rice paper to the background, which forced me to paint with very loose control over those areas. An added element of the torn paper other than the surprise is the texture it provides. Fine white lines show the white of the paper and emphasize the two musicians and their instruments.

Jazzy Duo
watercolor, 17 x 14

Karen H. Beach

redcloverdesign@comcast.net

Without a doubt, views and experiences while traveling, especially from islands in the Caribbean, provide the inspiration for the majority of my work. From time to time, it's a good idea to try something completely different and celebrate the beauty closer to home. This rose, called "Under the Tuscan Sun," graced my front porch for several summers. The rich glow of the blooms rivaled the sun itself.

Whatever the subject, my goal is to enhance the view – paying attention to the power of transparency, and keeping the painting fresh with pure and often surprising color. I'm drawn to unusual compositions, and unusual cropping, as well as interesting shapes of shadow and light.

I'm a big believer in watercolor "magic," whether it works for good - or not so good. Plan as you will, watercolor keeps you humble.

Tuscan Rose

watercolor, 8 x 11

Leigh Fulton

lrfulton@verizon.net

I particularly enjoy painting interiors because I like to imagine who lives there and what their story may be. I came upon a cozy bathroom in an old farmhouse in France and immediately knew I wanted to recreate the warm, inviting atmosphere created by the sun slanting in through the window and reflecting on the walls. In *Relaxation* I captured that warmth by mixing the paint directly on the paper and saving the white of the paper rather than masking. The golden glow made a nice contrast to the coolness of the tub, furniture, and linens, keeping the warmth the primary feeling in the room.

Relaxation
watercolor, 7 x 7

Regina E. Price

15115 Interlachen Dr., #717
Silver Spring, Maryland 20906
240-560-6957
301-502-3603 cell
hbrep@aol.com

Watercolor on canvas – not framed, but painted on the sides of the canvas. I did this painting in 2011, under the tutelage of Dave Daniels. It was a delight painting it.

Flower Display
watercolor, 28 x 36

Kay Fuller

158 North Carolina Ave. SE
Washington, DC 20003
202-547-5477
cfuller432@aol.com
KayandBobFuller.com

This is a mixed watermedia painting using watercolor and acrylic paint with paper collage and ink. The sky was boring in its original blue color, so I changed it to peach. This set the tone for the painting. I created much of the cliff by applying paint and spraying water to suggest crevasses and root effects. The collaged paper pieces enhanced this effect and added texture. The trees, originally shades of brown, were transformed when I added diluted gesso and laid strips of a plastic bag over the wet gesso. After the paint dried and the plastic pieces were pulled off, the trees had a bark-like texture. I repeated this technique on a couple of the rocks and created more texture with rice paper, hand-made stamps, and bubble wrap.

Abstract Landscape

watercolor, acrylic, ink, and collage, 14 x 19

Martha Allen

703-864-4784
mallen226@gmail.com

My paintings are a series of the disappearing landscapes and ways of life in western Loudoun County, Virginia. By researching and spending a great amount of time at the site, I hope to convey a real sense of place. In Loudon County, following General Sheridan's order in 1864, the "Burning Raid" left devastation and human suffering throughout the area; few barns and outbuildings survived the Civil War. Cumber Farm lies in the northwest tip of Virginia, with Dutchman Creek running through it and spectacular views of the mountains of Virginia, West Virginia, and Maryland. The barn was burned, but the house and dependencies were spared. The painting depicts the pig house and the side of the carriage house. Cumber Farm was named after the Armstrong family farms in Ireland and Charlottesville and is Gaelic for "little clod of land."

Survivors at Cumber Farm

watercolor, 11 x 15

Liang Wei

703-293-6311
mo_xiang_ting@yahoo.com
moxiangting.com

Before coming to the United States, Liang Wei studied Chinese painting at the Guangzhou Academy of Fine Arts. His adviser was Professor Fang Chuxiong. Liang Wei is a resident artist in the Torpedo Factory Art Center. In 2005 he received the Artist of the Year award, which is presented by The Friends of the Torpedo Factory Art Center, and he was awarded a solo show at the Target Gallery sponsored by the Art Center.

Liang Wei has exhibited his art in solo and group shows in museums and galleries throughout New York, Connecticut, Maryland, Virginia, and Washington D.C. He has won numerous awards including six Best in Show. In 2005 he placed First in Watercolor for Best of Virginia Artists and Artisans.

Beautiful Life

ink and color, 36 x 40

Carol Richardson Simmons

1403 San Rafael Place, NE
Albuquerque, New Mexico 87122
505-858-3350
clsimmons37@me.com

Maine Nest

watercolor, 22 x 30

Nothing in nature is as special as a hidden nest, whether it's in the crook of a tree or in a niche in rocks. Along the coast of Maine, many such nests tempt the eyes and cause wonder about what bird might hatch from the eggs. With these thoughts in mind, I created this painting in my studio.

Jill E. Poyerd

jpoyerd@yahoo.com
jpwatercolors.com

Old trees seem to have a character all their own, which is why I decided to present the tree in *Olde Grandeur* as a kind of portrait. I gave the tree center stage and played with the values in order to highlight the beautiful curves of the branches and its overall graceful form. The earthy color scheme also helped keep the focus on the shape and situation of the tree. As for techniques, I used masking fluid to preserve the white of the fine branches. The distant trees were implied through several glazes of wet-on-wet brushstrokes, and the foreground texture involved spritzing with water and then dropping in paint. *Olde Grandeur* was part of the National Watercolor Society's Annual Exhibition in 2011.

Olde Grandeur
watercolor, 24 x 18

Rob Henry

rah135@aol.com

Winter Morning

watercolor, 22 x 30

I just wanted to paint something that looked cold. I wanted it to feel like snow without resorting to the trick of putting salt onto the paper to make it look like snowflakes. The sky is many washes of three different blues and a subtle wash of purple. The real granular color is a paint called lapis lazuli that gave me the effect I was hoping for in the sky. I masked out the shapes of the roofs of the barns and then wet everything again while I floated in the background trees, keeping the line of the horizon nice and dry. I had originally planned for more trees along the road but am grateful that I stopped when I thought I was about 90 percent done.

Marie Baumann

snibbortoo@comcast.net

A trip to the Galápagos Islands off the coast of Ecuador in the Pacific Ocean inspired me to do a series of paintings based on the wildlife I encountered there. The Española mockingbird is endemic to the islands and is found on only one island, Española. Resembling our Northern mockingbird, it is cheeky and inquisitive.

This painting is on Yupo, a plastic that does not absorb the paint, but rather floats it on top of the page. My challenge was to control the paint in order to successfully render the shape, which I did with careful brushwork. I interpreted the feathers and shadows on the bird with soft pastel-like colors, and the lava rocks that make up the Galápagos Islands with blue-gray. I was happy to perfectly capture the uniqueness of this particular bird, which kindly flew right up to me for its photo!

Española Mockingbird
watercolor on yupo, 13 x 10

Ardythe Jolliff

191 Cardamon Drive
Edgewater, Maryland 21037
410-266-0744
jei@starpower.net

The painting *Autumn Blues* was inspired by a photograph I had taken during the fall season of several heads of kale at an outdoor nursery. The kale was an unusual color of dusty blue, and the bright afternoon sun created shimmering white light and colorful cast shadows. I cropped the photograph to showcase the center plant and drew the image on 300 lb. Arches bright white watercolor paper. I painted from left to right, light to dark, using glazes until I achieved the right values. I used masking to preserve the white areas and painted the background wet in wet. The color of the kale was so different that my usual mixture of transparent watercolors could not capture it. This gave me the chance to use my oft neglected paints, such as cobalt teal blue, cerulean blue, and peacock blue, in a mixture with other colors until I captured the unusual shades of the kale.

Autumn Blues
watercolor, 29 x 27

Jane S. Thomas

janesartstudio@yahoo.com

Towards the Light

transparent watercolor, 14 x 20

I spotted a woman walking through a dark alley into a sunlit courtyard in Old Town, Alexandria. When light hit her it created a powerful vibration around her opaque figure. Luckily, I had my camera in my hand to record this moment. I decided to do a painting of the scene with transparent watercolor on a half sheet of 140 lb. cold-press Arches watercolor paper. The challenge of this painting was to convey the drama, mystery, emotion, and mood created by placing dark objects against powerful light. I was satisfied with the outcome, and it won a best-in-show award in a juried exhibition.

Karin Sebolka

Loft Gallery
313 Mill Street, upstairs
Occoquan, Virginia 22125
703-490-1117
karinsebolka.com
valearts.com
loftgallery.org

For this painting, I placed magnolia branches in a large tub so that leaves, buds, and flowers looked as natural as if they were growing on the tree. On stretched paper I outlined the composition with a non-staining color. With a two-inch flat brush I carefully created the first layer on slightly damp paper, painting around the white magnolia blossoms. I decided on warm and cool colors, dark and light values, and sharp and soft edges. I love to paint behind the objects, which gives depth to the painting. If the color becomes too heavy, I use a soft natural sponge and clean water to bring back the transparency. The paper has to be dry before I start the process of glazing and between each layer of glazing. I prefer to paint standing so I can frequently step back from my table easel and see the composition as a whole. A way to notice mistakes in color and composition is to turn the painting upside down, which works as an eye opener for me. The painting should draw attention from about 10 feet away. Finally, I take the brush and look for the right spot to sign.

Maggie the Great
watercolor, 40 x 25

Deborah Pool Wurzel

dpwurzel@verizon.net

South Londonderry, Vermont

transparent watercolor, 22 x 30

A woman who lives along this road in Vermont commissioned this painting. I believe the ski hill in the distance is Bromley Mountain. What inspired me to paint this scene was the golden light on the trees contrasted with the white birches so typical of Vermont forests. Also, painting snow is one of my passions. I masked the white birches before beginning the washes. The trees were created by a careful layering of transparent color to build up the deep color of the wood. Painting snow, like painting any white object, offers opportunities to play with many colors and textures, depending on the kind of snow. All create worthwhile challenges.

Eleanor Cox

3980 Reed's Landing Circle
Midlothian, Virginia 23113
804-320-1445
804-513-7452 cell
eleanorcox@verizon.net
eleanorcox.com

Morning at Giverny

watercolor, 21 x 29

After teaching a June 2012 painting workshop in Provence, I joined the group of participating painters who extended their stay for three days in Paris. We immersed ourselves in the museums and cafes, concluding with an artists' trip to Giverny. The reference photo for *Morning at Giverny* was taken during that visit, my second time to see Monet's home and garden. I was just smitten with the lily pond, so lovingly tended by gardeners as if Monet himself were there. For the studio piece, I used Arches cold press 300 lb. paper and painted the entire piece upright. I used permanent rose and viridian for grays and greens, supported by quinacridone burnt orange, gold, aureolin, cadmium yellow light, cadmium orange, cadmium scarlet, cobalt, French ultramarine and manganese blue. Most of the painting was done with a #12 round Kolinsky sable brush. As an amateur gardener, I was absorbed by Monet's garden at Giverny that day, its allées, arbors, and roses. But my favorite was the lily pond.

Judelle McArdle

judy.mcardle@lifeanswers.com
judelle.com

One winter in Key Largo, Florida, I began to notice this mourning dove near the pool every day. The bird stayed close to the pool but somewhat tucked away in the foliage, waiting for lunchtime. Around noon the children would take a break from swimming to have lunch. They never seemed to be able to hang on to all of their French fries, dropping them everywhere all around the pool. And you-know-who would scoop them up. By the end of the winter the bird had developed a pretty broad backside - hence the name *Too Many French Fries*.

Too Many French Fries
transparent watercolor, 14 x 10

Emilie D. McBride

301-656-1359
edm3704@aol.com

On a January visit to a friend's farm in Vermont, I went snowshoeing in the early afternoon. Luckily, I had my camera with me because the sunlight on a pair of bare trees near her barn shone like polished metal. The snow intensified the light, and the shadows on the trees and the snow were vibrantly aglow. Once back home, I painted the picture and tried to capture the warmth of the winter sun on the scene. I used transparent rose, yellow, and blue for the snow shadows, and Winsor blue for the shadows on the trees.

Winter Trees
watercolor, 21 x 11

Patricia Givens

150 Preservation Circle
Pawleys Island, South Carolina 29585
843-314-3403
givenspatricia@sc.rr.com

The Peach Lady was an elderly lady I photographed at a local market on an island in the Seychelles. The younger members of her family were helping customers while she watched each transaction carefully. Her family would consult with her from time to time. To me, she represented wisdom that came from a lifetime of experience and an ability to instantly judge her customers' needs as well as their pocketbooks. I decided to paint a basket of peaches rather than the exotic fruits and vegetables that were on the table. Interestingly, I have had a number of people tell me that they had bought peaches from her at many different markets over the state of South Carolina.

The Peach Lady

watercolor, 21 x 24

Alice Webb

Ellicott City, Maryland
alicewebbsunburst@hotmail.com
alicewebb.com

The tropical Datura plant, often known as angel's trumpet, is plentiful in Central America. Its seeds are extremely toxic. I found this beautiful specimen when we were traveling through Costa Rica. The soft pink bells were set off by the complementary dark green. I masked the flowers with liquid frisket to give me clear space to build the green leaves from light to dark. I used sap green with mixtures of alizarin and indanthrene blue. I then removed the frisket and tinted the pink bells with green and pale yellow before building up mixes of rose madder and aureolin.

Pink Datura
watercolor, 11 x 12

Pemaquid Light

Harris C. Miller

322 Westview Court NE
Vienna, Virginia 22180
703-938-3575
hcmcmiller@verizon.net
HarrisMillerArt.com

watercolor, 15 x 22

For many years my wife and I travelled from our summer home in Wolfboro, New Hampshire, to visit the historic lighthouse at Pemaquid Point in Bristol, Maine. The lighthouse was commissioned in 1827 by John Quincy Adams and built that year. I used my imagination to create this *plein air* watercolor painting, rather than relying on a photograph.

67

Grace Rooney

gracemrooney@gmail.com

Under the Sea

watercolor, 10 x 14

This painting is on Yupo. When I first tried Yupo, I hated it. But I've found that the reason I hated it is now the reason I love it. It is unpredictable and you have total lack of control. When I begin, I have no idea what my subject matter will be. Part of the fun is to stamp objects into the wet paint and see what you get. Once my layer is dry, I observe the patterns. The path of the paint determines my subject.

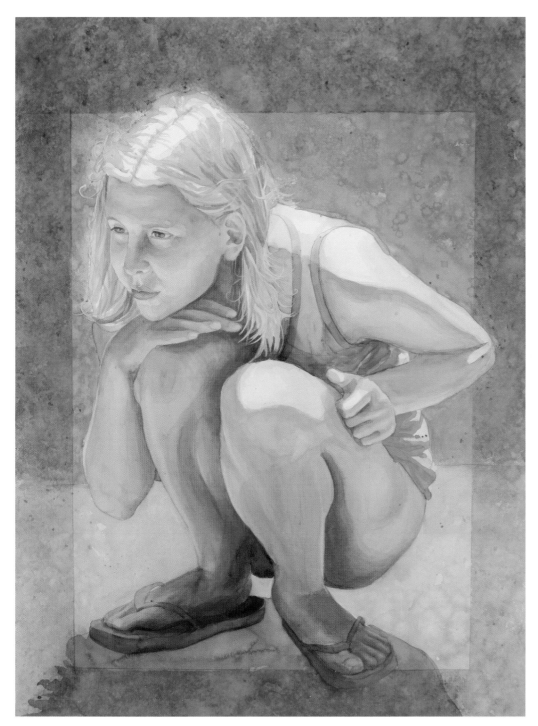

Margitta Hanff

marhanff@cox.net

I snapped this photo of a family member unbeknownst to her. My initial motivation was the unusual pose. It reminded me of a Maxfield Parrish illustration where the character is bent to fit in a box. It made me think of how hard some children try to "fit in the box" rather than celebrate their individuality. This is the reason for the indication of a box in the tightly fit composition. I did this by sponging on more paint around the box, which I just covered with a piece of mat board to keep the inside lighter. Later, as I was painting, I began to focus on that faraway facial expression that can be interpreted in a myriad of ways.

Zoë
watercolor, 29 x 21

Sue Moses

mmoses4@verizon.net
wmartists.com/moses/moses.html

In *Looking for a Handout,* I used a technique of pouring, spraying, and spattering paint in many layers without using my brushes at all. It is an involved and time-consuming process, which I swore I would never do again! Yet I have returned to it because it allows for the flow of water and mingling of pigment in a way different from brushwork.

A good composition and a good drawing are crucial to any painting, so I crop my reference photo to find the most interesting composition. Next, I make a value study and, finally, a color study. After transferring the image to the watercolor paper, I mask the areas to remain white. Using transparent watercolors, I begin pouring the lightest color first, working toward the darkest.

I then thin the paint with water and pour it on, tilting the paper to facilitate the flow of pigment. I spray some areas with water and again tilt the paper. These steps create a smooth transition of paint colors. I allow the painting to dry before proceeding to the next darker color. I find that it is important to be familiar with colors that mix well as you work toward darker values.

Looking for a Handout

transparent watercolor, 14 x 19

Wild Ginger

Lassie L. Corbett

703-435-1888
tripllcorbett@verizon.net
lassiecorbettart.com

watercolor, 15 x 22

Most subjects for my paintings come from travelling as a watercolor workshop teacher/adventure traveler. I begin my paintings with a series of on-location, detailed drawings of subjects that catch my interest, on good quality tracing paper. For travel purposes I carry a light backpack containing tracing paper, clips, tape, pencils, pens, eraser, a watercolor set, brushes, and a 7 x 10 wire-bound sketchbook for quick color sketches. The total weight is three pounds! In my suitcase I also have about 10 sheets of watercolor paper for painting opportunities. I take a few photos for color reference, but rarely draw from them. *Wild Ginger* was painted from five close-up drawings of ginger found on Hawaii. I rearranged the flowers in a cruciform design and masked out the white flowers. I then covered the paper with a glaze of aureolin yellow followed by a glaze of phthalo blue. When dry, a glaze of permanent rose was applied in areas. I applied continued washes of this triad to the leaves and flowers where needed.

Lieta Gerson

240-654-4736

When painting *It's a Party*, I felt it was speaking to me in the language of abstract art, a language of color harmonics, form, aesthetics, and equilibrium, between light and dark. There's nothing intellectual about my work. It is intuitive, leaving a vision on the surface for viewers to enjoy like a party.

It's a Party
watercolor, 30 x 22

Miyoko Mizuno

011-81-4-7103-1342 (Japan)
smizun10@reitaku-u.ac.jp

Peach & Quilt

watercolor, 29 x 40

My friend made a quilt for this painting at my request. The color of the quilt was so vivid that I chose peaches to better balance the overall color design. I have been painting a series of fabrics and fruits for 20 years and am always searching for new combinations. I would like to thank Deborah Ellis, Gwen Bragg, and Jane Simanis for my development as a watercolor artist.

Christine A. Heyse

301-680-9320
christineheyse@verizon.net
christineheyse.com

Church Ladies

watercolor, 15 x 22

This scene depicts some of the "babushkis," the elderly women in Russia who still frequent the churches, most of which were closed or destroyed during the reign of Stalin. This church, one of the oldest in Moscow, was the only one that didn't close. The ladies were coming out of the church on a very grey, rainy day, and I had only one chance to take a photo from quite a distance before they scattered. I had to crop and enlarge the photo a great deal and even converted it to black and white before I could see enough of the ladies to work from. I invented the colors, the puddles with reflections, and the snow. The original painting included the entire church steeple. When I had finished it, I didn't like it, so I brazenly cut it in half, eliminating the steeple altogether. Talk about cropping! Once the focus was on the ladies, the reason I had painted it in the first place, I loved it. This painting won an award in the Baltimore Watercolor Society Mid-Atlantic Show in 2005. It is in a private collection.

Susan J. Rubenstein

17049 Briardale Road
Derwood, Maryland 20855
301-330-9008
rubecarl@verizon.net

Anyone who has had the good fortune of living with and loving a cat surely recognizes their inscrutable, mysterious, independent ways. "What was the nature of my beloved cat Riley's dreams?" I wondered. Posing this question was my entry point into this painting.

Dreams can arise from one seemingly random beginning, and so did this composition. I started with Riley, in her chair "directing" where she might travel in her dream, and then the content of her narrative evolved. Extending the picture plane onto mat board provided the opportunity to expand the dream field and also play with complementary colors. It was the first time I painted with transparent watercolor on mat board, and I enjoyed observing the differences from working on cold press watercolor paper.

Riley has long departed, undoubtedly to kitty heaven. This *homage* to her was painted with great joy, which mirrors the considerable joy she gave to our family.

When Riley Dreams in Technicolor
watercolor, 17 x 14

Neyla Arnas

watercolorsbyneyla@hotmail.com

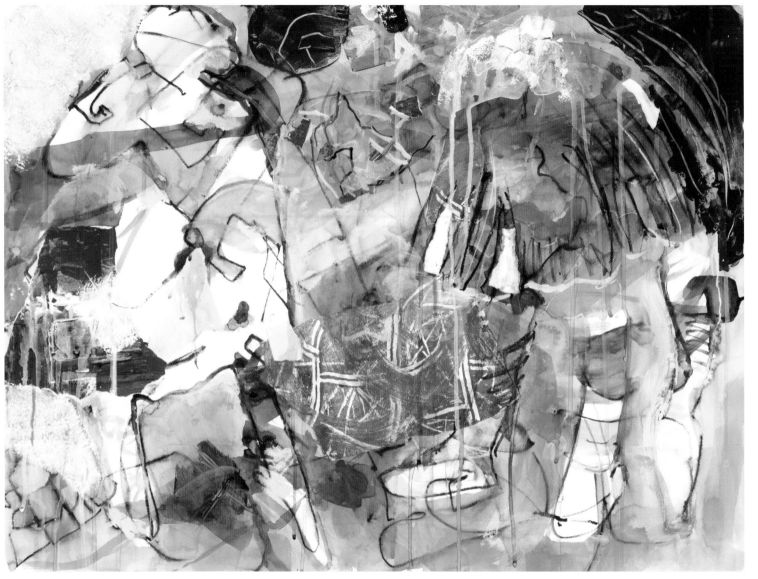

Riding the Steppes

acrylic, mixed media, 22 x 30

I love ballet; as a former dancer, I knew it was only a matter of time before I tackled the subject in painting. With color as my main focus, I paint intuitively, using a variety of tools and techniques to create interesting marks. I wanted to have some fun with this subject so I tried to capture movement and musicality rather than a photorealistic representation of the art form.

Dale Sheldon

dale@dalesheldon.com
dalesheldon.com

After returning from a week-long trip to Scotland, I found photographs I had taken with beautiful reflections in shop windows. The old buildings across the street were reflected in those windows, while store mannequins dressed in traditional Scottish kilts were also visible. I found another image of a sign with fish and the words "Old Fishmarket Close," which I layered over the original image of the shop windows. Once I was satisfied with the composition, I drew it in pencil on 400 lb. watercolor paper and decided on the color palette. The fluid acrylic process that I used on this painting requires masking in layers and working from light to dark. Once I achieve the desired hue, value, and intensity, I cover that layer with masking fluid to protect it and apply the next layer. When the painting is finished, masking fluid completely covers it and the image is hidden. Removing the masking fluid reveals the painting and is always exciting! Somehow the painting organizes itself in a way that is not apparent while I create it. Though the process is time intensive, the end result can be quite intriguing. But not all subjects are appropriate for this flattened, somewhat graphic look.

Old Fishmarket Close
fluid acrylic, 22 x 15

Jean K. Gill

JKGillWatercolor@aol.com
JeanKGill.com

I apply paint while the paper is dry and vertical, allowing color to run down the page and off the bottom. This procedure is a little risky but fun. I am fascinated with preserving the action of flowing watercolor in the finished piece. Gravity assists my brushwork, facilitating the downward movement of paint, and I encourage additional motion with occasional misting from a spray bottle. I paint the pine cones using complementary pairs of pure hues applied wet over wet to create interesting variegations within the neutralized colors. While orchestrating the process, I pay close attention to contrasts between adjacent areas, especially foreground against background, continually evaluating what degree of change to establish at each boundary. Should adjacent areas be analogous or dissimilar, warm or cool, bright or dull? I consider the quality of the edge sometimes, allowing adjacent areas to merge, blur, and flow, integrating foreground with background; other times, I use hard edges to create emphasis and separation. Painting can be a very cerebral pursuit, but too much planning can kill my motivation, so I use a mix of deliberation, improvisation, and exaggeration. I enjoy employing a strategy with options.

On Pines and Needles No. 2

transparent watercolor, 22 x 30

Charlotte Landis

landiscf@comcast.net

As an avid gardener, I enjoy working close to the earth. I stop and marvel at the distinctive characteristics of mushrooms I find while planting and pruning in Alexandria, Virginia. In *Fun Guys,* I achieved a dreamlike quality by painting in bold colors, close-up, and omitting any distraction but vibrant color in the background. Sketching first from real life, then photos, I accomplished the depth and personality of the underside of the mushrooms' gills by allowing the white of the paper to set off the deep shadows. The mushrooms came to life with exaggerated detail and bold color. It is with humor and an acute appreciation for nature that I transformed fungus into *Fun Guys.*

Fun Guys
watercolor, 21 x 14

Muriel Ebitz

301-519-6998

During a visit to the Brookside Gardens hothouse in Rockville, Maryland, I noticed how many of the tropical plants had patterns of lines that were repeated over and over again. The idea for a painting took hold, and I quickly snapped at least a dozen pictures.

The shapes of the plant took form without much change, but I knew the challenge would be the repeating lines. After carefully drawing the stems and each line on the leaves, along with the shapes of the leaves, I covered each line with masking fluid, allowing me to paint the leaves, flowers, and dark background shapes without disturbing the patterns I had created.

After removing the masking fluid, I painted the patterned lines with colors that would give contrast or subtlety to adjoining colors. The dark background color helps to delineate the strong leaf shapes.

Patterns
watercolor, 26 x 17

Carroll M. Stone

5029 Grand Cypress Boulevard
North Port, Florida 34287
llewelyn137@comcast.net

In Full Glory

watercolor, 5 x 8

The subject of this painting is a colorful succulent, the desert cabbage, which I admired at the Garden of Five Senses near my home. The painting focuses on the fleshy leaves, their repetitive circular shapes, and the graduation of color and perspective. The newest leaves, located at the center of the succulent, stand erect and are pale in color. As the succulent grows, the change in perspective reveals a gradual progression from elongated elliptical to oval to nearly circular leaves. Affected by environmental factors, the color of the leaves intensifies through this progression. As the plant matures it reaches its full glory, causing the casual observer to pause, admire, and appreciate the full character and richness of the plant. Perhaps there is a correlation between this succulent and the mature person – people are ultimately identified by the character and colors of their lives, which reflect their growth as individuals.

81

Jane Cordes
Simanis

janecordes@gmail.com

Gus

transparent watercolor, 14 x 21

Gus is my Maine coon cat, who joins me and my students in the studio when class is in session. He usually wanders in, often stops to say hello and get a scratch here and there, and then retires to his favorite den of pillows in the sitting room next to the studio. What a picture! And I had my camera ready. I used mask on Gus's whiskers; otherwise, the painting is trickless, just straight transparent color.

Mary Allen

13012 Deer Ridge Road
Culpeper, Virginia 22701
540-825-3102
maryballen1@gmail.com
maryballen.net

Time for Tea was the signature piece for my solo show entitled "Garden Party!" The show was a salute to my love of vintage clothes, spring flowers and social events in the garden. It was intended to create the colorful, carefree, yet civilized atmosphere of a time not long past when visiting meant face-to-face contact, an unhurried pace, and reflective musings among the flowers.

Time for Tea
watercolor, 18 x 18

Margaret Mather Pearson

(MAGZ)

703-360-8790
magzjewelry@gmail.com
magzwatercolors.com

The Robert Morris Inn

watercolor, 15 x 22

One of my favorite workshops was at the Robert Morris Inn in Oxford, Maryland.

This is a view of the second floor with the bright afternoon light shining through the window.

I used transparent watercolors on Arches watercolor paper. I never use black from the tube. I make my own grays and blacks mixing burnt sienna and different blue paints. The color is so much richer.

Jane McElvany Coonce

4057 North 27th Street
Arlington, Virginia 22207
703-524-7049
www.jmcelvany.com
jmcelvany.blogspot.com
jane.coonce@verizon.net

This was a painting I did over an unsuccessful painting.

For the first painting I put two coats of gloss medium on one side of a piece of Aquarius II paper, letting it dry between coats. I created an image using pthalo blue, ACRA magenta, and yellow orange azo. However, the original painting was unsuccessful. So, with the same palette, I painted over the first version. Then, using water-soluble crayons, I drew a new image. I painted the city lights negatively around the figures and the umbrella. I loved the results, and it was much better than the original one underneath.

Under My Umbrella
acrylic and water-soluble crayons, 14 x 10

Susan Herron

sherronart@yahoo.com
susanherron.com

The light fell beautifully on this young woman and seemed to highlight her dewy freshness. After doing a compositional value study, I chose to use an abstract acrylic underpainting. Then I lifted the lights with alcohol. I painted a warm background to balance the cool darks and the blue bandana. This approach seemed to capture what I hoped to say about Chelsea.

Chelsea
acrylic, 19 x 19

Ellen F. Delaney

edelaneyart@gmail.com
ellendelaneyart.com

This scene shows a simple country house against a blue starlit night sky. It was painted in October, when the orange and gold fall leaves influenced the choice of color for the abstract landform and the harvest moon. The colors create a mood rather than a realistic scene. I applied the paint with a palette knife to 300 lb. paper. I began by covering the entire sheet with the blue of the sky. The bits of blue that show through the ground plane help unify the painting.

Night Sky

acrylic, 18 x 23

Marilyn Feldman

11300 Crossing Glen Court
Potomac, Maryland 20854
301-294-0321

Artfully arranged objects of art or a jumble of antiques – window displays are meant to engage the viewer, just as a good painting does. As I stop to view a storefront window, I recall the still lifes created by my instructors at the Corcoran School of Art in Washington. I am flooded with memories of paint-spattered classrooms, the pungent aroma of turpentine, the smear of oil paint, the dust of charcoal and pastels, the scrape of easels on the floor. This shop window drew me in with the graceful curves and intricate patterns of imported vases. There is just a hint of the carved screen and flower arrangements that complete the window display, a ready-made still life.

Chinese Vases
watercolor, 30 x 22

Yolanda Frederikse

9625 Dewmar Lane
Kensington, Maryland 20895
hyfred@verizon.net

African Violets

watercolor, 22 x 30

African violets bloom profusely on the windowsill in my art studio. They called out to be painted with the morning sun spilling over them, and it was indeed the light that colored them and gave them form. I drew directly on Arches paper very lightly with pencil, soaked and blotted the full sheet of paper, and began to paint. I worked the whole day on the image, from time to time adding touches of glaze to enhance the delicate veils of color on the violet petals and the furry leaves.

This watercolor was exhibited in a Potomac Valley Watercolor show in Virginia and is now in a private collection in Japan.

Ruth Ensley

9008 Fort Craig Drive
Burke, Virginia 22015
703-503-8462
rensleyart@yahoo.com

While living in Costa Rica for five years, I made many forays into the tropical forest to see exotic flora and fauna. I am told that there are more than 26,000 orchid species in the world, and many of these exist in Costa Rica. The spider orchid is one of the more unusual species, and for that reason I was drawn to working with the design.

I like best my paintings where I have pushed the reality of what I am painting into some abstraction of texture, shape, and, at times color. I think it makes the subject appear and feel more real. I don't want this to be too obvious, for I want the viewer to look closely to see the abstractions of texture and shape. For many years I have worked with collage and been fascinated with different textures. This fascination spilled over into the way I use watercolor. I have also found that watercolor is the perfect medium to paint the lush transparencies, textures, brilliant colors, and piercing light of tropical forests.

Spider Orchid

watercolor, 29 x 32

By the Creek

transparent watercolor, 13 x 20–

Graciela Congote Keane

gckeane@hotmail.com
gracielakeane.com

I visited this secluded place during a vacation in northern Pennsylvania. Its light, quietness, and multitude of greens attracted me. I first did a very simple line drawing, indicating areas of lights and shadows and main masses and clumps of trees. I then poured colors, letting them run and mix; while the colors mixed I took care of keeping certain areas clean, such as the side of the trees receiving the morning light. This required cleaning the color and re-pouring, until I saw the effects I wanted. When the paper was drier I went back to define certain forms and details to finish the painting.

Carol
Vorosmarti

301-340-7326

Catching the feeling of sunlight with back lighting was my main objective in this painting. I placed my plants in a south-facing window one winter's day, and after sketching them in I laid down a wet wash of colors that I would use later in the painting. The amaryllis had to be drawn a foot shorter then it actually was to fit it in the composition. Some of the colors I used are lost to me now, but I'm sure permanent alizarin crimson and a transparent yellow were involved in the blossoms. I used brown madder to paint negatively around the begonia leaves, and a touch of turquoise made the painting pop. I've tried to duplicate the hard and soft edges in the flower petals in other watercolors without success. I'm happy it worked in this one.

Winter Flowering

watercolor, 21 x 27

Jack Harding

hardingarts@gmail.com

This painting stems from a spring trip to Pike Place Market in Seattle. The market was full of wonderful bunches of tulips, and I took many pictures directly into the tulip blossoms. This has resulted in two series of paintings, one colored *(Spring Fling)* and one using the limited, Velazquez palette *(Spring Elegy)*.

I believe that the limited palette of yellow (raw sienna), orange (burnt sienna), Payne's grey, and lamp black provides an interesting perspective on the flowers and tends to makes the shapes more abstract and organic. Furthermore, I attempted to lead the eye through the painting by the abstract patterns of lowest value (yellow) and greatest value (black). I used transparent watercolor on distressed rice paper for this painting. I crunched dry rice paper into a ball, then moistened it, spread it out, and glued it onto watercolor paper. The distressed paper has many small cracks and blemishes, leading to textural effects when the paint is applied.

Spring Elegy 2
watercolor on distressed rice paper, 28 x 19

Kathryn Grill Hoeppel

hoeppelfinearts.com

Autumn leaves float in a breeze that, despite the piercing morning rays, carry the first licks of winter's chills. It's the first hard frost of the season.

This abstract combines elements of transparent watercolor, ink, and collage. I gave special attention to composition, and drawing before painting allowed the range of values to help lead the viewer's eye. I added small collage elements to contribute extra texture and depth and to reiterate the overall design of this piece.

Autumn's First Frost
watermedia and collage, 30 x 22

Gloria Logan

gloria.logan@mac.com
torpedofactory.org

My recent work explores remixing visual stimuli that are compelling to me. The painting begins in an intuitive way and becomes more structured as it develops. For me, painting is about discovery, abstraction, and creation. Through the process of accumulating, changing, and layering, I strive to create a surface of great variety and richness.

You may find the influence of some of my favorite painters in my work. They include Hundertwasser, Klee, Klimt, Bonnard, and Vuillard.

The Gods Must Be Crazy

mixed media collage, 22 x 30

Nellie Chao

10500 Rockville Pike #120
Rockville, Maryland 20852
301-897-5408
nelliechao@gmail.com

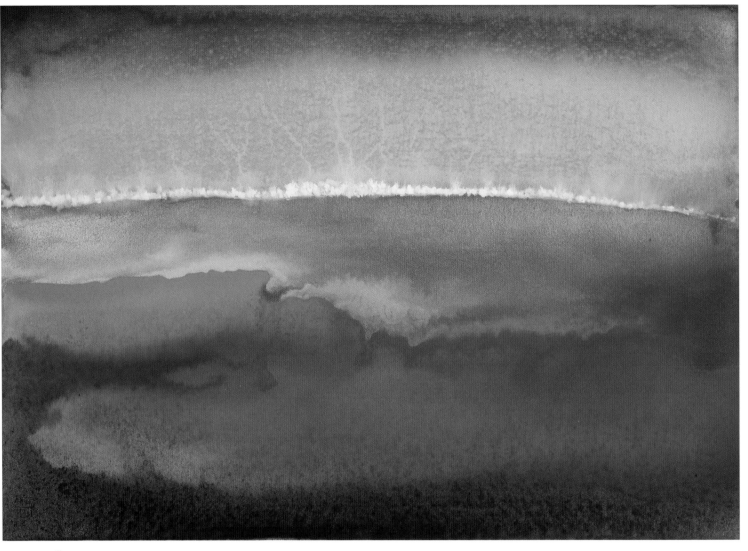

Primal Energy

watercolor and gouache on gold Shikishi board, 14 x 20

PoMo, or "splash ink," painting is an ancient Chinese technique, though the results look contemporary. In the case of using watercolors, thickened watercolors are poured onto gold or silver leafed "shikishi" board. I manipulated layers of color with brushwork and by tipping, allowing them to blend and bleed.

Primal Energy was one the few PoMo paintings I did without any preconception as to what the end results would be. I had no images, no thoughts in my mind, except for the colors that I desired to use. Almost at the end, suddenly I had the impulse to pour a thin white line where the orange and gold colors met – I then stopped and here is the piece.

Rosa Vera

118 Via Finita Street
San Antonio, Texas 78229
210-451-8041
rositavera@aol.com
rosavera.com

A flower girl at my nephew's wedding on a brisk March day provided the subject of this painting. The sky was bright with intermittent clouds and sun. This piece took me nearly a year to finish, and the title evolved with the work itself. I put gold gesso on watercolor paper and painted with gouache. Although it was easy to wipe the paint off the gessoed surface, making corrections was difficult in that an entire area might disappear and need to be painted again. This piece won First Place in the Over 60 Art Competition 2012, *The Artist's Magazine.*

Into the Light
gouache, 21 x 21

Liz Roberts

jrliz@msn.com

Sum of the Parts is a painting that began as I start all of my abstract paintings: thick paint brushed on paper, forming random shapes, with no particular design in mind. I blend with a roller and scratch and rub with a palette knife, sandpaper, blade, anything that can make a mark to reveal the underlying colors. Surprises come to the surface, some not as interesting or appealing as others, so they are covered up with more paint. I spend a long, enjoyable time experimenting with color and texture, and then one composition stands out and is particularly appealing. The mood of the painting evolves spontaneously, requiring some line work with water-soluble crayons, inks, and stamps and the finishing touches of collage to establish a focal point. Some areas are retextured and touched up with paint and line to complete the painting. The addition of collage pieces from an old math book gave this painting its title of *Sum of the Parts*. It has been in several shows and won awards, and viewers are invited to interpret the contents in a personal way, much as my personal expression developed it.

Sum of the Parts
acrylic collage, 20 x 20

Lisa Gillispie

lisagillispie@earthlink.net
lisagillispieart.com

People are among my favorite subjects, both interesting poses by complete strangers and intimate looks at family members and friends. *Contemplative* is an interpretation of my daughter, Ilene. I painted her using an acrylic technique that starts with an abstract underpainting, adding transparent layers and then carving around the underpainting to create her figure. One of the enjoyable qualities of acrylic painting is both using this transparency and mixing with white to create opaque areas.

Contemplative

acrylic, 11 x 14

Pauline Davis Lorfano

402 Old Courthouse Road, NE
Vienna, Virginia 22180
703-938-8539
pd14art@aol.com
PaulineLorfanoArt.com

On my annual painting trip to Maine, these particular lobsters were in the kitchen sink with the kitchen light emphasizing the beautiful darks of the shells. I took numerous photographs of this energetic group and made a sketch. From the sketch came the painting. It received an Honorable Mention the first time I showed it. I again painted on it and put in an extra lobster (upper left). This time it earned a Third Place prize. I painted on it yet again, emphasizing the darks and color design, and now I feel it is complete. In 2007 it won Second Place in the "Food for Thought" exhibit at the Mansion at Strathmore Hall, in Rockville, Maryland. Since then I have left it in its frame — no more painting.

I entered it in the 30th Anniversary Exhibition of the American Society of Marine Artists and it was accepted. In two years it travelled to five museums on the East Coast. The exhibition catalog and write-up have been accepted by the Library of Congress.

Maine Attraction

watercolor, 22 x 29

Outskirts of Town

watercolor under acrylic, 9 x 12

Traci Oberle

traci@ilovewatercolors.com
ilovewatercolors.com

An old watercolor painting serves as the starting point for *The Outskirts of Town.*

Wearing latex gloves, I extract acrylic paint from the tube and rub it onto the paper with my fingers. I use isopropyl alcohol on cotton swabs to soften edges or create a scratchy effect.

I disregard impulses to plan ahead or to have any preconceived notions of how the painting should look when it is finished. I want to keep my mind focused and react to what is happening on the paper. Each action drives the next action with the hope that intuition is guiding the process. I try to be spontaneous and let go of ideas about perfection. I paint over and around shapes to enhance the quality of the surface. When the page is nearly covered, I read the composition for areas that suggest further development reminiscent of an object or landscape.

Anthony (Tony) Neville

5521 North 23rd Street
Arlington, Virginia 22205
Tonyneville01@gmail.com
tonyneville.net

Georgetown University

watercolor, 12 x 16

Evening light along the Potomac has inspired a series of paintings looking across the river. A new palette, derived from a recent workshop, prompts use of new mixes such as brown madder and indigo. The vantage point of the waterline lends emphasis to the Flemish gothic buildings.

Betzi Robinson

autumnmoonstudio.com

This work is done on unsized rice paper with sumi (Asian ink) and Chinese watercolors. It is part of a series I did on trees. I chose the cherry tree during the annual Cherry Blossom Festival in Washington, D.C. I was impressed by the beauty of the efforts to blossom put out by the older trees. More of the tree's trunk and branch structure is visible in the older trees than what one sees in the newer, more resplendent younger trees. To me it was a kind of metaphor for the possibilities of old age.

Old Tree in Spring Finery
sumi-e and watercolor, 15 x 13

Deborah Marshall Elliott

dmelliott@cox.net
ViennaArtsSociety.org

Oftentimes I choose to paint something in order to learn how to paint it.

This beautiful grouping of irises was planted under the stained glass windows of a little chapel in Lancaster, Pennsylvania. During my morning walk, they came to my notice because of the way the light illuminated the paper-thin petals. The red and yellow beard that peeked between the standards (upper petals) and falls (lower petals) of the flower, as well as the colors and hues I discovered throughout the painting process, were delightful surprises.

Fleur-de-Lis
transparent watercolor, 19 x 12

Sand Beach

watercolor, 12 x 16

Yolanda Koh

Columbia, Maryland
443-956-1656
yolandakoh@comcast.net
yolanda-koh.fineartamerica.com

Maine is known as the "Land of Vacations." My husband and I discovered Bar Harbor, in Acadia National Park, on our vacation last fall. The rock formations of Sand Beach are simply stunning and mesmerizing. Although it was an overcast day, the rare beauty of these outcrops was not dampened by weather. I carefully planned the approach for this painting, deciding to paint each rock shape with a local color. I first glazed the rocks with a neutral shade. Then I added other colors, one at a time: pink, orange and purple, while the neutral paint was wet, so that each shape would have color and light variations. After the paint was dry, I took my time detailing each rock by outlining with a rigger or a Chinese brush, varying the line weight and splattering, giving each rock a unique character. It was like the brush dashed and skipped from rock to rock, articulating its intricacies. I delighted in painting these rocks and loved the milky quality of the waves washing over them. The gentle waves hit the seashore with a soft flapping sound that day. What a serene and peaceful feeling.

Madeline Wikler

12520 Davan Drive
Silver Spring, Maryland 20904
301-622-3019
madwik@aol.com
madelinewikler.com

I captured these three guys in front of a pub in Ireland several years ago. I managed one snapshot before they saw me and the mood was lost. They seem to represent perfectly their time and place, and I hope the painting does so as well. I tend to work with three transparent primary colors, and in this image I poured an initial light wash of alizarin crimson, raw sienna, and Winsor blue. I masked and poured successive layers, and finished by directly painting the three figures.

Cheers!

transparent watercolor, 16 x 21

Marilyn Milici

6205 Berlee Drive
Alexandria, Virginia 22312
703-941-4575
mjmilici@aol.com

High in the Andes I encountered this rag tag bunch of musicians rallying the spirits of hundreds of exhausted pilgrims on their way to a religious site. What they lacked in ability they made up for in enthusiasm. I was moved by the spiritual experience but also intrigued by the shadows their instruments cast and the arc created by their positions.

I chose three colors from among a collection of free samples I rarely use: Maimeri Berlin blue, Schminke ruby red, and hansa yellow. I masked and poured, masked and poured at least six times using all three colors each time. By the last pour I had a sorry-looking mess, but when all the masking was removed I was pleasantly surprised.

La Banda
watercolor, 30 x 22

Marni M. Lawson

703-577-0967
marnilawsonwatercolors@hotmail.com
marnilawsonwatercolors.com

"Please step 100 feet back from the water's edge!" warned the ranger at Schoodic Education and Research Center in Maine, where I was Artist in Residence in 2011. He told me of a woman who was lured to the geysers of water where the ocean swells meet the granite coast.

With lapdog in one hand and cell phone in the other so her caller could hear the wild surf, she was swept into the ocean, never to be seen again.

This painting emerged as a kind of cautionary tale in honor of that unknown woman who forgot, for a few critical moments, the unyielding power of the ocean.

Warning!
watercolor and gouache, 15 x 11

Peggy-Ann
K. Duke

8210 Murphy Road
Fulton, Maryland 20759
301-498-1175

I have been studying oriental brush painting for at least 25 years with several teachers. This is a sumi-e painting in the *Ling Nan* style of southern China painters. My current teacher, Henry Wo Yue-Kee, is an internationally recognized artist of this style. As a trained botanist and botanical illustrator, finding this style of painting with watercolor was a wonderfully freeing experience!

Visiting the Banana

watercolor, 16 x 19

Elaine
Weiner-Reid

elaineweinerart@gmail.com
elaineweinerart.com
elaineweinerart.blogspot.com

Working without a net – every day and every painting is one decision followed by another decision and another. Each painting begins after a lot of thought and with the determination to be true to my own style and vision. It is about creating something that does not already exist. Each is a unique adventure, an exploration, with all the challenges and wonder that entails. Like me, my art is a work in progress. My art is my passion, and my intent is to be true to myself and that passion.

Lucid dreaming, daydreaming, nightmares, and stream of consciousness play key roles in my body of work. Taking insomnia where it leads, I explore the intersection between conscious, sub-conscious, and unconscious thought. Dream fragments remembered or documented intersect and mingle with thoughts and intuitive decision-making. Life experiences, relationships, and creative works like *L'Alchimiste* by Paulo Coelho continue to inspire and influence my creations.

Légende Personelle

mixed media on canvas, 16 x 20

Christine Lashley

lashleys@mail.com
christinelashley.com

Favorite Fish

watercolor, 12 x 18

I like the challenge of painting fish and moving water. When I saw these trout at a fish pond in Vermont, I knew I had to paint them. I was disappointed that my reference photos were so average-looking when I reviewed them, so I used my memory for the colors of the fish and the water. Most of the painting is done with minimal layers to preserve freshness. I used no masking; I prefer to paint around shapes, letting them reveal themselves.

Yoshimi S. Matsukata

301-320-7681
yoshimi2@verizon.net

Exuberance

transparent watercolor, 20 x 30

I was drawn to the hosta plant mostly for the strong structure of the plant itself: the rigid stalks and the waxy thick leaves with deep veins. The prominent veins in the leaves remind me of blood vessels and veins in our own bodies, pumping blood and nutrition throughout our system. It fascinates me to see the visual similarities between the human circulatory system, which radiates from the center of our body to our extremities, and the vascular system in a plant. I titled my painting *Exuberance* because, to me, the hosta leaves in this painting represent a strong desire to live. The leaves face and reach for the sun, seeking light, creating nutrition, and growing larger and stronger to receive even more light. I feel the energy and quiet strength of nature in the hosta leaves.

Amy Thompson

amygthompson@msn.com

In order to capture the ephemeral magic of a light-filled morning I chose to use a limited palette of analogous colors with just a pop of their complement. The vines and leaves are an interweaving tangle of light and shadow as backdrop to the magnificent but fleeting display.

Glorious Morning
transparent watercolor, 18 x 13

Patricia N. Porter

pporter3art@gmail.com

There are times when you just have to paint something – an expression, a scene, a favorite place or memory. I painted this portrait of our family pet, a wonderful little rescue. He is a sweet but bossy little guy. Here he is telling me that it's time for a walk. I love to paint portraits of animals and people, with a focus on the eyes and facial expression to communicate mood and emotion.

Mr. C
watercolor, 5 x 5

Pat Leibowitz

3712 Leland Street
Chevy Chase, Maryland 20815
301-654-6177
pleibowitz@yahoo.com
patleibowitz.com

This is a scene that I saw and loved in the Jewish quarter of Venice. A young child stood with her mother at one of the old fountains and seemed captivated by the shape of the water streaming over her hands. I thought about the scene for quite a while and decided to paint it in watercolor. I poured in the background with rose, hansa yellow, and phthalo blue around all the masked light areas. I painted the figures directly, emphasizing the child. I often do a combination of pouring and direct painting and I feel it gives a more luminous look to the watercolors.

Water Play
watercolor, 29 x 22

Jeanne Thornhill Ulrich

7713 Oxon Hill Road
Oxon Hill, Maryland 20745
ulrichart@mac.com
ulrichart.com

Naptime

watercolor, 22 x 30

While vacationing with our daughter's family and friends in Clerac, France, I entered the room to find daughter Diana and grandson Findlay asleep on the couch. I managed to get my camera and capture the scene without waking them. This image became a full-sheet watercolor, painted after we returned home. The tartan over the back of the couch is the family's Gunn plaid.

Jane S. Jordan

1010 Prince Street, Apt. 4
Alexandria, Virginia 22314
janemcnivenjordan@gmail.com

Dordogne Kitchen was painted from a series of photographs I took at Petite Rousset, an 18th century French farmhouse. This was a shadowed interior with strong light coming in the French doors and pouring over the old terracotta floor. Using primarily warm colors, I had the most difficulty with the yellow back wall, which was in shadow. By repeated glazing I knocked it back sufficiently to balance the door light. The view through the doors I kept warm, but minimal. I lifted with a damp brush to depict the light streaming onto the floor. To shadow the red tablecloth, which had cadmium red in it, I glazed over it with permanent magenta.

As a vendor at the Old Town Alexandria Farmers' Market, I sell reproductions of this painting, which continues to be one of my most popular.

Dordogne Kitchen
watercolor, 20 x 15

Elaine S. Hoffman

6839 Wilson Lane
Bethesda, Maryland 20817
202-841-0270
elaineshoffman47@gmail.com

I am a psychotherapist by vocation and very interested in people. This interest carries over into my love of art and painting, and as a result, many of my paintings try to capture the little moments while people are going about their day. Almost all of my paintings are based on photographs I have taken as I wander about. I photographed *Serenade* at the Beaux Arts Festival at the University of Miami in Florida. While walking throughout the campus and the booths, I noticed a man dressed in all white, playing the fiddle as he jumped and danced around with contagious energy, entertaining people as they walked about browsing the art.

Back home in my studio, I composed and sketched from my photograph onto Arches full-size (22x30), 140 lb. paper. My intent was to apply the watercolor as opaque rather than as transparent and add some touches of caran d'ache for accents. I wanted a more impressionistic style rather than a focus on detail, and thus purposely omitted detail in the facial features. This fiddler, originally dressed in all white, was transformed in the painting into a symphony of color! I emphasized color changes rather than value changes, with the hopeful intent to "serenade" you through the painting!

Serenade
watercolor and caran d'ache, 30 x 22

Linda J. Sherman

P.O. Box 83832
Gaithersburg, Maryland 20883
ljsherman13@gmail.com

I love to visit Brookside Gardens every season of the year and always come across beautiful plants and flowers that inspire paintings. This colorful pot of flowers called to me with its vibrant reds and oranges. I loved this point of view, looking into the open flowers from above. I used many glazes of color until I felt the flowers were as vibrant as they appeared in the pot.

Joyful Potful

watercolor, 27 x 42

Judith Gray

judiesbulldog5500@verizon.net

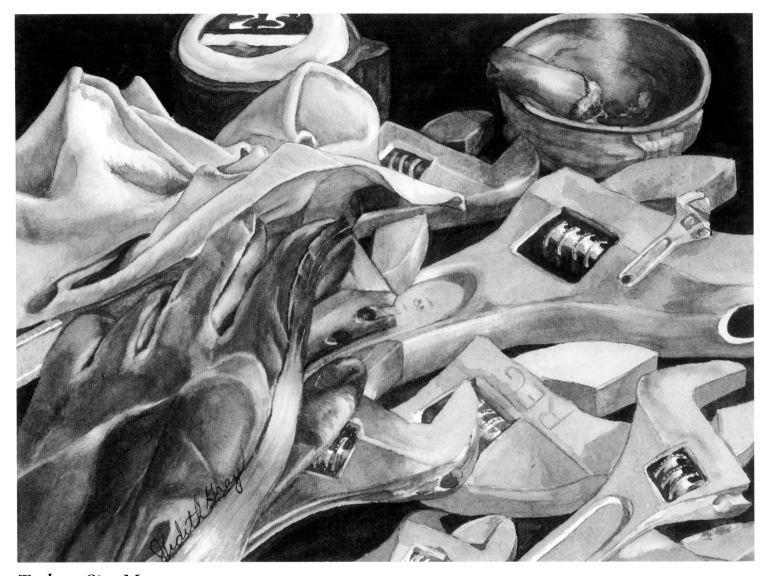

Tools — Size Matters

watercolor, 8 x 11

Morning light slipped into our garage where my husband was starting
his next project, and the edges of those tools sparkled, asking to be
painted. After the first few sketches I decided that the tools needed their
own color. And the combination of light red and cerulean gave them the
hints of shine and rust!

Teresa Kramer

8212 Cindy Lane
Bethesda, Maryland 20817
trsk4@aol.com

This egg tempera painting was commissioned by a Florida homeowner who made an open-ended request for me to "paint something." As soon as I saw his woodworking shop I knew there was subject matter with meaning for us both. In his 80s, the owner was no longer actively using his shop, but he had made some remarkable pieces there. Through the doorway, light was diffused over the seemingly mundane tools and equipment in a way that suggested that they were the source of some deeply satisfying outcomes. To carry out that theme, I used egg tempera (on clayboard) because it can be used in rich, fluid layers of color enhanced by the light coming through. Egg tempera takes patience, but in this case I was easily propelled by the idea that had prompted me to begin the painting.

Butch's Workshop
egg tempera, 16 x 12

Linda H. Kirvan

lhkirvan@aol.com
lindakirvan.com

Skipjack Icon is presented in a vertical format to represent the strength of the massive sail that was used to power these historic sailing ships as they harvested oysters from the Chesapeake Bay. Transparent washes capture the bounce of light and shadows formed by the giant folds of the slack sail in sunlight. I used wet into wet and glazing techniques throughout the painting. The emphasis is on the sail, while the sky, ship, and horizon are painted more simply and are only used as a foil for the center of interest. I used photographic references to capture the complex folds and rigging.

Skipjack Icon
transparent watercolor, 30 x 22

Betty Ganley

bettyganley@hotmail.com
bettyganley.com

The painting was finished. In a carefree moment I decided to take the risk of adding a more dramatic finishing touch or — ruining it completely. I rewet the foreground water area, let it sit for about one minute, and then dragged a thirsty, but damp brush through the water in receding, curved stripes to produce realistic ripples. Success!

Gulls and Dinghies

watercolor, 15 x 22

Marni Maree

marnimaree.com

I visited Petra, Jordan, last year. Although the red rock-cut city is truly one of the many great wonders of the world, I was just as fascinated by the camels I met. I did not ride one but took many photos of them, trying to capture their decorations and their expressions. Since this guy did not spit at me, I was able to paint him with a very pleasant personality. I have painted and sold many camels since this one. Somehow they are both regal and comical at the same time.

Ride to Petra
watercolor, 11 x 7

Meg MacKenzie

megmackenzie1@verizon.net
megmackenzieart.tumblr.com

The past few years I have returned to the subject that I started drawing as a youngster, the majestic power of the horse. Usually I begin each painting with an underpainting, texturing, or collage. Then I look for a horse or horses to appear and develop an image. *His Majesty* began as a collage of pieces from a damaged painting. I experimented with various placements of the torn pieces and began rotating the paper until the image of the horse spoke to me and I saw my subject. The painting evokes an incident that occurred when I was 12 or 13 years of age.

His Majesty

watermedia, 21 x 28

Marcia Gladsky Esquibel

570-275-0275
moonflower47@verizon.net
northmountainartleague.com

I have lived and painted in the beautiful Susquehanna Valley of central Pennsylvania since 2007. Prior to that, my husband, Augusto, and I lived inside the Beltway for 30 years. We vacationed in more than 40 countries and participated in artist workshops in France, Mexico, Egypt, and the United States. We visited both fine art and folk art wonderlands, absorbing, photographing, and appreciating. Inspiration for my work comes from those memories and pictures. Inspiration also comes from everyday life experiences and the great beauty that God placed in His creations.

I paint mostly in transparent watercolor on paper or with casein on a variety of prepared surfaces. When I paint, I enter another plane of being, losing all track of time. I do not get tired or hungry, and I am completely absorbed by what appears on the painting surface. I will sacrifice technical purity to preserve the emotion that provoked the painting. In my head I hear the lessons of teachers.

Warmed by the Sun

transparent watercolor, 14 x 20

This painting was a gift for my husband, a psychiatrist and physician for 57 years, who always liked bulls. The penetrating gaze of this bull reminds me of his penetrating gaze into the minds and hearts of his patients and how he warmed their lives with his compassionate care.

Elinor Morley

esmorley@aol.com

In my estimation, the challenge of Yupo paper is not in conquering it with heavy paint and careful washes, but following the illusions created by color and water on this seemingly uncooperative paper. I enjoyed allowing Yupo to dictate my painting journey.

Swamp Dog came about when I swiped a damp tissue over an unsuccessful landscape painting. I had intended to make a lake or pond and to add trees and rocks. When it dried, there remained a spot that looked like an eye, untouched, on the left side of the white shape. With one stroke, I added the nose, another stroke the space between the legs. Then the other eye and a base of water shapes and *Swamp Dog* appeared. This took about a minute, the rest of the scene many hours of fun. Pushing and pulling and adding colors, I developed a composition from the abstract shapes already there, giving the piece a sense of mystery.

Yupo paper gave me permission to enjoy a happy accident.

Swamp Dog
watercolor, 11 x 8

Connie Boland

bcboland@aol.com
bcboland33@gmail.com

I have always loved Queen Anne's lace. It grows wild at the beach – even in the dunes. It is difficult to paint with the white on white and the daintiest of tiny blossoms forming the delicate flower. I used a lot of masking fluid along with negative painting to achieve the blossoms. The pine trees and bushes set it off. I am always challenged by Queen Anne's lace and love painting it.

Queen Anne's Lace
watercolor, 21 x 14

Summer Strollers

Rosemary Nothwanger

2060 Brownstone Lane
Charlottesville, Virginia 22901
434-974-6638
sekiar27@gmail.com

watercolor, 20 x 28

One hot summer day while walking along the C & O Canal, I found it was delightful to spend a long walk in the shade of the big trees alongside the canal waters. The deep shade held wonderful dark colors, and the dappled sun made attractive patterns on the path and clothing of the people. I enjoyed painting this picture because I felt it conveyed the atmosphere of a hot day being enjoyed by the cool strollers. My sources were photos I took and notes on the colors in the sunshine and shadows.

Judy Antico

703-354-5613
pantico@mindspring.com

I have traveled in many parts of the world, from Alaska to Namibia, and take great enjoyment in the beauty of the earth's varied landscapes, which are often the inspiration for my paintings.

This intuitive painting began with a few gestural lines and shapes and the sense that the composition would finally turn into a landscape. As I worked on the piece, many triangular shapes emerged, and I added paint layers to try to create an interesting, more active painting without changing the original shapes.

After setting the painting across the room for a few weeks, looking at it from time to time, I decided I needed to balance the composition with a strong vertical, which I added in the shape of the orange trees. While this unexpected "imaginary landscape" is just that, corresponding to no particular place, I believe it has nevertheless been informed, like many of my other works, by my abiding love for the colors, shapes, and wonders of the natural world.

Imaginary Landscape

acrylic, 21 x 27

Linda E. Maldonado

lindamaldonado@aol.com
LindaMaldonado.com

This painting is one of a series I began with the notion in mind of exotic gardens in ancient Persia. I've found that holding a theme or location in my mind while I paint helps guide the development of the painting and the choices I make. This is especially helpful when working on abstract pieces for which I don't have a specific sketch or detailed plan at the beginning. I planned a palette of warm colors on the first layers, followed by rich dark paint as I felt the painting near completion. To prepare the canvas, I glued rice papers and tissue paper in a random fashion, sprayed them with water, then floated yellows and reds over the wet surface. Once it dried, I began defining the shapes and values.

Persian Garden: *Winter Stars*
acrylic & collage, 24 x 18

Marjean Willett

marjeanwillett@gmail.com
marjeanwillett.com

Birdland

transparent watercolor, 22 x 30

Birdland is a transparent watercolor that was part of a series based on random washes. In this case I did a quarter-sheet study, starting with overlapping gray washes. The bird shapes started to appear and I encouraged them, finishing with the colors and black. I enlarged this image to a full sheet, using tracing paper grids, and made it tidier. I moved one bird whose legs were emerging from another bird's head. This painting and its companion piece sold quickly.

Mary Eggers

eggersm@ix.netcom.com
maryeggers.com

What can I say? Merlin likes to sit
under the umbrella when it's drying!
This piece was a beach project
just in case it rained while visiting
friends north of Lewes, Delaware.
It's a collage using pieces of acrylic
underpaintings, and the white
areas are the watercolor paper.
The only actual painting I did was
to apply a transparent red over the
underpainting, which gives it color
variation as the darker tones of the
underpainting show through.

In Case it Rains
acrylic collage, 15 x 15

Sally H. Olson

703-724-7646
s.olsonart@gmail.com
sallyolsonart.com

I have painted this piece five or six times as I love the subject matter, and I like this version the best. I began by drawing the large shapes and then masked everything that wasn't water. I let it dry for 24 hours. Using washes of fluid acrylics, I floated in layers of colors, texturing the surface when the paper was cool, and letting each layer dry thoroughly before doing another. Once I established color and some depth, I removed the masking fluid and worked on the rocks, marble, and Koi with several washes of transparent and semi-transparent watercolor, keeping everything at the same level of development.

When only the details on the objects were left to do, I turned my attention back to the water area and added more depth and shadows with both watercolors and fluid acrylics.

To protect each layer, I sealed it with a thin acrylic wash and let it dry thoroughly. Once the painting neared completion, I set it aside for a few days. With fresh eyes, I made adjustments and added the finishing details.

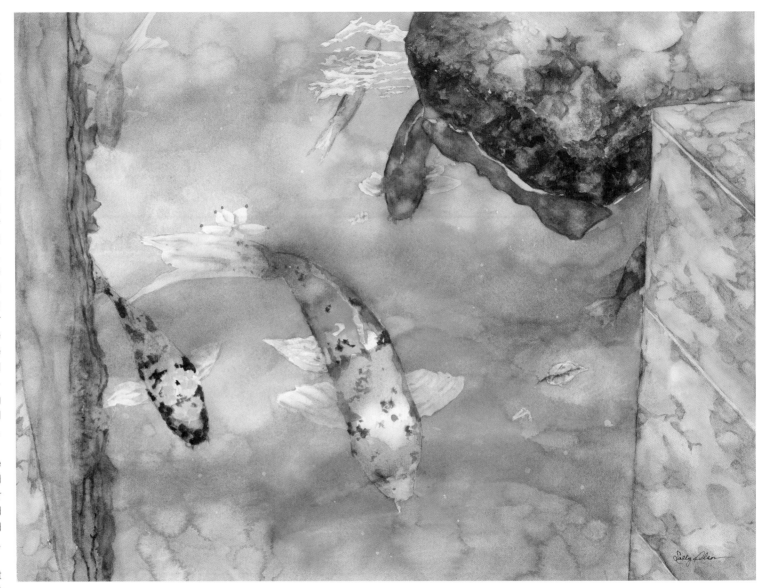

Narrow Passage

watercolor and acrylic, 18 x 24

Brenda C. Barthell

bcbart@verizon.net

My paintings are the result of both planned and intuitive processes. Initially, an image may pique my interest and I will make a thumbnail sketch or re-invent it as I paint. However, the original source is transformed as I move in and out of abstraction, layering and editing the images that please or challenge me. It is only when the painting has some personal meaning that I feel ready to sign my name to it.

The city of Chicago, my first home in the United States, inspired this particular piece. I juxtaposed vertical elements of urban architecture with strokes of color to represent a river, park, or lakefront that evoked fond memories.

The Lake Effect
acrylic, 18 x 18

Sarah Andrews

sarahwearsblue@gmail.com

On a trip to Scotland, I was struck by the way the light burst through a clerestory cathedral window. Using a variation on a technique taught by Lee Weiss, I randomly toned both sides of a sheet of torchon paper and then flipped the damp paper on a slick surface to more evenly distribute the "randomness" and bring some cool colors into warm areas and vice versa. The texture captured both the feeling of the old stonework and the dust floating in the air. Light areas were lifted out with a sponge and additional texture added as needed by spraying water onto both wet and dry surfaces. Allowing some of the color to be random and pre-toning my paper free me from the compulsion to match my color choices to reality.

Paisley Cathedral
watercolor, 23 x 18

Chris Engnoth

703-582-9899
chris@cengnoth.com
cengnoth.com

Thing-a-ma-bob

transparent watercolor, 11 x 15

I have no idea what this piece of machinery is. I was on my way through West Virginia, driving to my daughter's wedding rehearsal, looking for old farm equipment. I came around a bend in the road and found a farm equipment graveyard filled with machinery that was rusting to pieces. The deep rust colors contrasted with the moss and lichens encrusting these old tractors. I tried to play with the warm and cool colors, blending them on the paper and being careful not to lose the texture by glazing over too much.

Jane Gott

janegott@verizon.net

Ocean Breezes

watercolor, 14 x 20

This painting reminds me of a month I spent in Kauai. One of my favorite parts of each day was to watch the light dancing on the hammocks as the sun slowly set on the sea and the mountain range on the far right. I tried to capture this play of light in my watercolor *Ocean Breezes*. I did not want to become obsessed trying to paint every string in the hammock; I wanted to use a painterly approach and let the viewer finish the hammock pattern created by the negative space. I was interested in presenting the hammock in the foreground, hinting at the ocean and mountain view in the background. To me, this painting is about the wonderful moment when all seemed quiet and relaxed, and the ocean breezes called me to enjoy the sea and distant mountain. For this painting I used transparent watercolors and a limited palette and left the whites. I painted on Arches cold press paper.

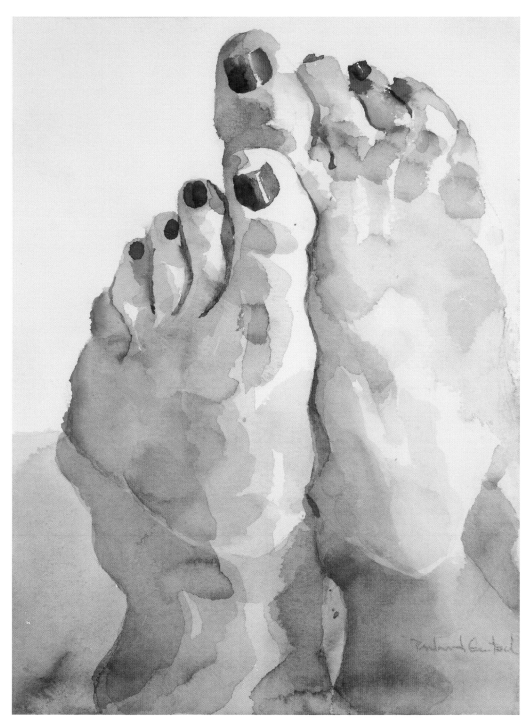

Fae Penland

fae@faepenland.com
faepenland.com

Oh my, I have loved looking at my feet. Anyway, what can I say? This watercolor was done in the tub.

Ten in the Tub
watercolor, 12 x 10

Deborah Brisker Burk

301-762-5655
debby@artvistas.com
deborahbriskerburk.com

This is the last painting in my *Femalescape* series. Abstract shapes dominate the field. The chunks of space are divided in varying sizes to heighten the movement across the page. The figure is transparent and integrated into the composition, not as easily recognized as in the preceding art works, as different waves of color weave in and around her. This piece acts as a transition, or bridge, hence the name, between figurative and abstract styles in my ongoing process.

Femalescape IX — Transition
watercolor, acrylic, watercolor pencils, pastel, 26 x 20

Ya Gotta Laugh

Therese (Terri) Rea

118 Gresham Place
Falls Church, Virginia 22046
703-237-7683
terrirea@mac.com

This self-portrait reflects my artistic evolution from working in transparent watercolor to acrylic paint.

I have always been fascinated by human nature, by how we develop both as people and as artists over the life cycle. My own artistic process has involved accepting a personal style that is quirky and intense. I have enjoyed the more intuitive and painterly style that acrylics allow.

acrylic, 14 x 18

Elise Ritter

703-731-5744
eliseritter@yahoo.com
eliserittergallery.com
Elise-Ritter.fineartamercia.com

Cindy's Café

watercolor, 16 x 20

This painting was created after a trip to a Sonoma, California, wine country town, with my best friend and her elderly mother. I wanted to show the golden sunlight of a late afternoon and highlight the lights and darks of the intense shadows. Café scenes have always fascinated me because of the interplay between the abstract forms of the umbrellas, the light, and the shapes of the people at leisure, usually laughing and animated or relaxed and contemplative. Color is at the forefront here, too, with the warm reds, yellows, and corals contrasted with the complementary greens of the trees — and the yellows and purples as well. I like to tap into the emotions of a special day spent with beloved friends, and the feelings and happiness we shared. *Cindy's Café* was accepted into the 2012 Virginia Watercolor Society show. My sincerest thanks to the artists of the Potomac Valley Watercolorists, the Northern Virginia Art Center, the Arlington Artists Alliance, the Virginia Watercolor Society, the galleries and art leagues of Virginia's Chesapeake Bay Northern Neck/ Middle Peninsula region, and friends, family, and other supporters along the way.

Barbara Sullivan

11471 Meath Drive
Fairfax, Virginia 22030
703-278-8145
bsullivan90@gmail.com
bsullivanart.com

This painting is a collage incorporating acrylics, acrylic inks, and gesso. I used illustration board coated with gesso as the support. I stained white tissue paper with acrylic paints and inks and allowed it to dry. Then I glued pieces of the stained paper to the support using matte medium. The challenge was trying to arrange a good abstract composition with no reference material. A beneficial aspect of this technique is that mistakes can be covered with gesso and more tissue paper glued on top. Once started, the piece took on a life of its own. I had no preconceived idea of how it would turn out, which was liberating and exciting. I just kept gluing the pieces of colored tissue paper using compositional rules as I progressed. I had 90 percent of the papers glued on, then stopped to analyze the piece. I decided to continue the orange off the bottom edge and added a few dark areas in the top third of the painting. Once it was dry, I coated the entire piece twice with a 50/50 mix of matte and gloss medium, allowing the first coat to dry before applying the second.

Meandering
acrylic collage, 15 x 11

Shelby Conley

202-256-6956
shelbyconley@gmail.com

This little sparrow flew onto a railing very close to us as we were enjoying the view at Lake Atitlan, Guatemala. No matter how much we moved or talked, he was unfazed and as openly curious as a small child. As this was painted with a very limited palette, I concentrated primarily on keeping a light hand to portray the fluffiness of the feathers. In contrast, the bold, A-shaped composition seemed a good match for the cheeky attitude of the young bird.

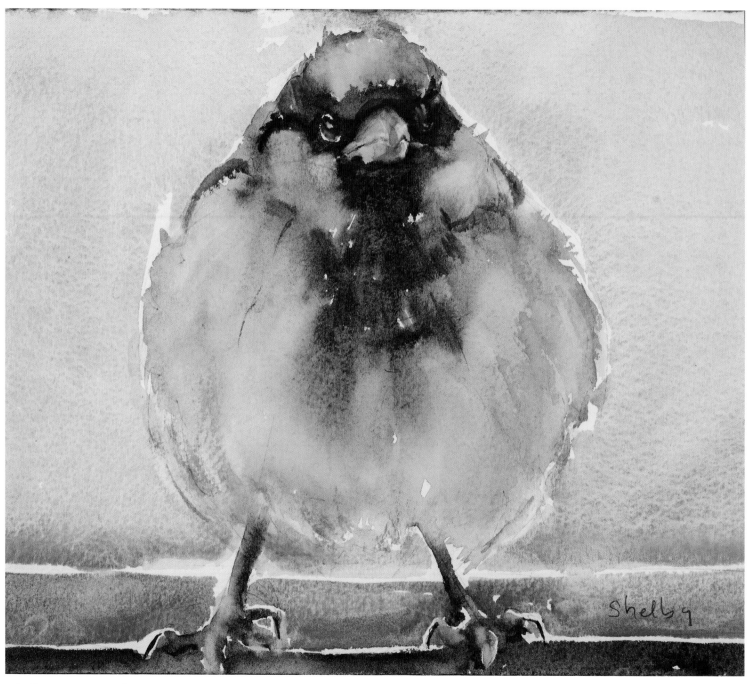

A Curious Bird

watercolor, 8 x 9

Julie A. Smith

301-570-0416
spottedpony2@juno.com

Raven Blues

acrylic, 18 x 24

Throughout history, people have regarded crows in many different ways – as messengers, or spirit guides, or totems, or even bad omens. I love to observe them. They project a wisdom beyond my knowing and a mastery of their world while being at one with it. I painted *Raven Blues* with the same intent as all my works depicting living things. I wanted to express my respect and belief that there are no lesser beings. All creation is graced and blessed, and I am grateful to participate in the dance of life.

Patrick Roth

10214 Eagle Landing Court
Burke, Virginia 22015
703-250-0641

Day is Done was started during the summer at Orkney Springs, Virginia. I wasn't satisfied and abandoned the painting. The following winter I got the painting out and decided to finish it. Perhaps it was memories of long soft summer evenings at Shrine Mount that encouraged me to take up the painting again. Anyway, after I finished it I circulated a copy by email to my large extended family. Not too long after that, when we visited my brother for dinner, my sister-in-law had a copy on her refrigerator door. Of course, it graces her living room wall today.

Day is Done
gouache, 10 x 7

Carolyn Grossé Gawarecki

grosseart.com

Escapement

watercolor with casein, 22 x 30

On one of my many trips to New York City, I snapped this tenement building standing starkly against a clear sky. It had an interesting red fire escape casting shadows on a rough brick wall. I proceeded to paint the picture in my studio by scraping a palette knife over the rough paper using a mixture of casein and watercolor paint. I was listening to a Garrison Keillor program, so while scraping in some remnants of posters on the wall, I was inspired to paint in parts of a Powder Milk Biscuit poster to commemorate the occasion. I gave the sky several glazes of a strong blue-green to complement the red tones in the building. I then added some white accents for the ever-present pigeons.

Painted on rough 140 lb. Arches paper with Winsor & Newton watercolors.

Nancy Walnes

703-369-3806
nwalnes@comcast.net
nancywalneswatercolors.com

...Not Far from the Tree

watercolor, 14 x 11

Tackling this still life excited me because of the many contrasts. The bright sunlight outside gave the trees a ghostly quality against the strong, cool shadows of my inside work space. The apples and bowl were dense with color, and their smooth surfaces and the glass table against the rough brick surface created contrasting textures. The contrasts also had an architectural aspect with the round apples, the oval bowl, and the square windows and surrounding rectangular shapes. Finally, contrast occurred in my handling of the watercolor. The background was a light, soft wash, while the bowl was an almost out-of-the-tube mixture of alizarin crimson and thalo blue. I painted the bricks wet in wet from several different reds and a splattering of blue. Lifting, scrubbing, and layering were all part of the process. The bite out of the apple has its own story. For years I have hoped to harvest apples from my trees, but the squirrels have always picked them clean and strewn the half-eaten remains.

Toni Bragg

tonibragg@comcast.net
tonibragg.com

I was inspired by bananas I saw in Guatemala growing "upside down" — I had no idea they didn't grow in the direction gravity would seem to take them! There are such interesting shapes and colors in the bananas, stems, and surrounding growth. I used a pouring technique, protecting the light values with frisket and layering in the darker values with each pour of color. The result was very pleasing to me; there is a mood to this painting that I think makes the bananas rather majestic.

Gone Bananas
watercolor, 21 x 11

Peggy Talbot Wagner

4800 Fillmore Avenue, Apartment 1354
Alexandria, Virginia 22311
571-312-7384
fairdirect@aol.com

A perfect, sunny day and a delighted Grandpa Chappie watching his grandchildren cavort in the swimming pool were all I needed to inspire me to paint a larger work than usual.

Poolside Spectator
watercolor, 21 x 15

Judy Wengrovitz

5220 Cather Road
Springfield, Virginia 22151
703-256-4683
swengrovit@aol.com
judyswatercolors.com

The Crossing

watercolor, 22 x 28

I enjoy the challenge of using my watercolor to capture a complicated New York street scene. I photograph my scene carefully to get a good composition. I look for yellow cabs, lamp posts, signs, people, store fronts, and traffic signs. To simplify, I paint all areas with similar colors at the same time. First I mask off any white or lighted areas. Then I paint all the reds in the scene, all the yellows, and so forth. Finally, I paint the tall buildings and the people. I save small details for last. I try to simplify when painting such a busy, complicated scene.

Donna Sturm

donnaesturm@gmail.com

Summer Still Life

transparent watercolor, 17 x 23

This painting was inspired by the still-life paintings of Giorgio Morandi, a 20th-century Italian artist whose work I have long admired. His compositions are truly mystical, imbuing humble, simple forms with a transcendent beauty. The Phillips Collection in Washington, D.C., owns a number of paintings by Morandi and hosted an exhibit of his work in 2009 titled "Morandi: Master of Modern Still Life." During the exhibit, the gift shop at the Phillips Collection featured a number of objects reminiscent of the simple forms of muted color that Morandi often used in his paintings. The beige vase and the bowl containing strawberries came from the museum shop.

Cathleen F. Gardner

gardnercf@hotmail.com

The painting *Duet* was inspired by spider mums but evolved into a completely imaginary pair of flowers painted with Chinese watercolors on white silk. I began by using a very light tan wash for a minimal sketch of the subject, but then the painting took on a life of its own as it went along. The silk comes already mounted on a paper backing, which is then dry mounted onto foam core prior to painting. The Chinese watercolors come in the form of small dried chips, powder, or sticks, and I use only Chinese brushes. The petals on these flowers were a particular challenge. I painted each with multiple thin layers of watercolor blended carefully into the tips, which I tinted with white. I lightly painted the leaves with only one or two layers of color. Although I use Chinese materials, I enjoy experimenting with them and consider my work to be too varied to be thought of as traditionally Chinese. *Duet* was awarded an Honorable Mention in the PVW Green Spring Gardens show of 2009.

Duet
Chinese watercolor, 13 x 11

Marie Kaneko
Shaughnessy

1200 Allendale Road
McLean, Virginia 22101
703-893-8116
markaneko@aol.com

Plum Blossoms with Bird

sumi-e (ink and watercolor), 12 x 18

Plum Blossoms with Bird is painted with watercolors mixed with sumi ink to delineate the main trunk and branches of the plum tree. This partial statement is a method used in many oriental as well as western-style paintings. The plum blossom is a favorite of painters because it is hardy, the blooms emerging in late February in Tokyo while the weather is still quite cold. Imagine the drabness of late winter brightened with the blossoming of these lovely flowers, so that even the sparrows that winter over quickly find their place among the blooms.

Cuties

Chinese ink and watercolor on rice paper, 12 x 31

Irene Tsai

1312 Titania Lane
McLean, Virginia 22102
703-288-0423
ireneluu@yahoo.com

Cats are my favorite animals. I used Chinese ink, watercolor, and rice paper in this painting. I used a fine horsehair brush to create the fluffiness of the kittens' hair. Each kitten shows a very different character and personality, and they are all very special.

Elaine Nunnally

elainenunn@aol.com

My cat, Gracie, often enjoys sitting up on the ledge of a shelf in my bathroom next to an antique vase that was hand painted by my grandmother. On this particular morning, the light from the window was shining brightly on her and the vase, and she was in a restful pose, her head down and enjoying the warmth of the sun. Gracie's soft fur next to the hardness of the shiny ceramic vase was a study in contrasts, not only in texture, but in color as well. Sometimes you experience a moment in time that is a painting just waiting to be painted. This was one of those times.

I did this on a half sheet of Arches cold press paper, using traditional watercolor methods. Then I used an atomizer to spray orange acrylic ink over the gray of the walls to bring more warmth to the overall painting. Look closely and you will see it.

Gracie and Grandmother's Vase
watercolor and acrylic, 22 x 15

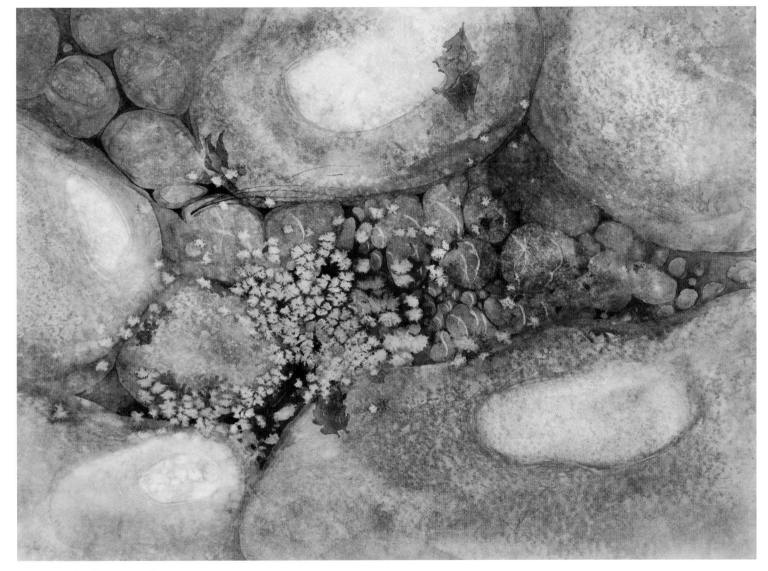

Beneath the Surface XV

Gwendolyn C. Bragg

703-780-0868
gwenbragg@aol.com
gwenbragg.com

watercolor, 21 x 29

This is the 15th in a continuing series of paintings of rocks under running water that incorporates a technique I learned from Lee Weiss. The process creates textures and unique color mixing that I find particularly appropriate for certain subjects such as the rocks. This painting was awarded the Potomac Valley Watercolorists Prize in the Art League's annual 'Scapes show in 2011 and the Bronze Medal in the Southern Watercolor Society Show in the same year.

Concetta C. Scott

1111 Dead Run Dr.
McLean, Virginia 22101
concetta.scott@verizon.net

This painting is the second in a new series of florals in a large horizontal format. The series explores followers of a same large family, showing the differences in the varieties of color, size, foliage, and root system of each bloom. The composition is designed to support, unite, and enhance each flower. The addition of items such as bees and bugs are part of the irises' environment. I spent many an enjoyable day at Mrs. Thomas Iris Farm sketching. That gracious lady was most patient with the visiting artists. Looking out at the hundreds of colorful irises was like seeing an earthbound field of rainbows. The research I did for this watercolor painting was an enriching and learning experience for me.

Irises Are Rainbows

watercolor, 16 x 20

Jacqueline Saunders

9519 Wythal Lane
Burke, Virginia 22015
703-323-5263
703-403-1793 cell
jackieink@verizon.net
jackiesaunders.com

Alexis is a young woman full of vitality, enthusiasm, and good humor. Her personality is colorful and cheerful and her skin tones are just as vibrant. I chose to paint her with brilliant pigments.

Alexis came to our studio several afternoons and I painted her from three viewpoints each day, seeking to capture her infectious spirit. Rather than beginning with a basic mid-value skin tone and developing form with accurate shadow shapes, I began painting the light-struck area with a bright mixture of cadmium red and raw sienna. I left highlights of white paper, and moved into shadow with a mix of cadmium red and French ultramarine blue. In the cooler areas I added permanent rose or carmine to make violet darks.

The totality of nine heads, looking intently in various directions, the intense color, spots of light and calligraphic brush strokes all contribute to a lively description of Alexis's youthful spirit. Painting her was pure delight.

Wonderful Moments with Alexis
watercolor, 27 x 23

Carol Bouville

cbouville@aol.com
carolbouville.com

For a long time I have been wanting to successfully bring a still-life floral painting into being using primarily my intuition. I believe it is easier to paint abstractly when one has no agenda, but in this case I did have a goal in mind.

I began, as I do for many of my "abstract-ish" paintings, by wetting a full sheet of Fabriano soft press (Artistico), 300 lb. paper and dropping in bright hues of acrylic ink such as crimson and turquoise. Knowing I wanted to express floral shapes, I tried to save lots of white places where the inks and the water could mix in a soupy way to keep the mood upbeat. I repeated this process several times, introducing texture as I went along, while creating flower shapes by painting negatively. When I was satisfied with the overall shapes and patterns of light and dark (or not!), I introduced pre-stained and decorated rice papers to build up the surface, creating texture and repeating patterns and colors.

I had fun creating this painting and hope the viewer enjoys the experience as well.

Whimsy
mixed watermedia and collage, 30 x 22

160

Debra Grayer Halprin

301-260-9701
halprinart@aol.com
halprinart.com

Kensington Station 2011

acrylic, 26 x 36

Color! Color! Color! I love color. Can you tell?

Each year I organize an art exhibition over Labor Day Weekend in the Town of Kensington, Maryland. To participate in the show, each artist must submit at least one painting representative of an area within the town. In the painting *Kensington Station 2011,* I use my love of color to depict the train tracks next to the station that has been the centerpiece of the town.

I use liquid acrylic to achieve the vibrancy that I enjoy. I begin by pooling water into the area to be painted. I then drop the acrylic paint into the area and let the water do its thing. To achieve the interesting shapes within each area, I drop more water. This creates blossoms and tonal value, which add interest to the piece.

Jamaliah Morais

703-893-1509
703-683-5250 studio

Fragrance of Peonies

ink and watercolor on rice paper, 18 x 33

In Oriental brush painting, the peony is widely regarded as the Queen of Flowers. It symbolizes not only beauty but also wealth and distinction. When peonies bloom, it has been said that their perfume spreads for a thousand miles and also attracts butterflies. Folklore has it that the butterflies symbolize the young man and the peonies symbolize the young girl. When the peony begins to bloom, it is picked by the young man.

My aim in this brush painting is to depict the spirit of the peonies and even the fragrance of these glorious flowers, not just the physical resemblance of the flowers. I endeavor to capture the essence and spirit of these peonies by weaving a tapestry of exquisite lines, colors, and shades. In so doing, I strive to create both harmony and a poetry of nature that will breathe life into and give special meaning to the painting.

Loy McGaughy

2165 Cabots Point Lane
Reston, Virginia 20191
703-758-9566
mcgaughy2@verizon.net

While the initial inspiration for *Wild Roses* came from personal photos, the final composition combines imagination and representation. I melded the subject matter of several photos, added embellishments, freely modified the colors and cropping, and rotated the shapes. I used Caran d'Ache water-soluble crayons to break up the background and enhance the blossoms for a more abstract look. My goal was to create a painting that moves beyond what can be captured with a camera.

Wild Roses
watercolor and water-soluble crayons, 15 x 11

Mary Phelan

703-309-4621
themaryphelan@gmail.com

Midnight Magnolias

watercolor and acrylic, 19 x 28

I often think of my garden as a collection of "models." Working from life adds energy and immediacy to my painting and encourages me to take advantage of watercolor's potential to be both vivid and delicate. Magnolias are a favorite subject and the colorful hearts of the Saucer Magnolia are especially fun to paint. This painting was annoyingly long in the making. I painted the magnolias, intentionally leaving the exposed paper as the background, hoping for a minimalist, Asian feel to the

image. After months of dissatisfaction and feeling that the painting looked unfinished rather than minimal, I began exploring ideas to finish the work. After several disastrous attempts, I had almost given up the painting as ruined. One night I saw this black and gold background in a dream. I love juxtaposing geometric shapes with organic subjects, and the black and gold had the Asian flavor I had originally intended.

Terry Anstrom

703-201-7649
tanstrom@cox.net
watercolors-byterry.com

The Big Red Tulip was juried into a National Gallery West Show. I wanted the focus to be the heart of the tulip, so I painted a close-up of the center, emphasizing the dark black pistil with contrasting yellow and white. Normally, I paint the outside petals first. In this case, I wanted the interior of the flower, with the rich contrast, to be central to the composition. I mixed Winsor green, alizarin crimson, dioxazine violet, and French ultramarine blue to create the dark black hue. Various hues of red, yellow, blue, and purple created brilliantly colored petals and shadows.

Big Red Tulip
watercolor, 30 x 24

Sarah Gerould

703-622-7569
sgerould@gmail.com
sarahgerould.com

I have always been intrigued by the marvelous line of Toulouse Lautrec and wanted to paint something in his style. A fight scene with gourds seemed just the ticket. I also enjoyed working the pun on his name and on the French words in his poster into the title of this piece.

Gluttons for a Fight With Nothing to Lose
transparent watercolor, 20 x 16

Monna Kauppinen

301-434-4753

California Gold

transparent watercolor, 7 x 10

I sometimes carry a small box of watercolors with me on my travels. The limited palette often dictates my choice of subject, forcing me to think in new ways about inspiration and creativity. In this painting I was pleased with the crispness I achieved, especially in rendering the complex blossom.

This work led me to portray California apricots and poppies in later paintings.

Into the Meadow

watercolor and ink on rice paper, 17 x 36

Frank H. Spink

5158 Piedmont Place
Annandale, Virginia 22003
spinkfrank@gmail.com

I painted *Into the Meadow* with watercolor and ink on rice paper. I started as a watercolorist using 400 lb. Arches paper, so this combination of traditional sumi-e East Asian painting materials was a dramatic change for me. As a trained architect, I was used to drawing and then painting. That method is not possible using thin rice papers. Rather than starting with color washes, my first direct painting is a drawing with hand-ground ink. Color is added later, and can be applied on both sides of the thin rice paper. My composition does not follow Asian traditions of composition, but uses Western perspective with significant distortion of scale in elements like the tree and the sun. My objective is to establish myself as a crossover painter, combining Western art methods with personal interpretation of Asian painting traditions.

Ginger Sanaie

7336 Eldorado Street
McLean, Virginia 22102
H – 703-356-3428
C – 571-205-6127

This painting was done from life using India ink on watercolor paper. After a few preliminary pencil marks, I sketched the model using a black Micron pen. I premixed several values of ink and added ink on top of the pen drawing. This painting did not take very long, but it was done at the end of a session that had lasted several hours. I was warmed up, but the model was clearly a bit tired. Later, I was tempted to make changes, but I resisted the urge, and left it alone, as a record of my perceptions that particular day.

Relaxed
ink, 11 x 6

Peter B. Ulrich

ulrichart@mac.com
ulrichart.com

Brittany Clam Diggers

watercolor, 14 x 21

When the tide recedes in southern Brittany, miles of estuary are exposed. The locals know the tidal schedule and flock to the sands armed with buckets and rakes to dig for cockles. I joined them one sunny morning in August, not only to dig the delicious *fruits de mer*, but also to snap photos for painting references. I combined several of these for this *contre jour* study. My intent was to capture the brilliance and sparkle of the morning light. I also took advantage of the artist's prerogative to alter the scene by strategically placing tidal pools, using them as mirrors to reflect the clam diggers. We had about two hours to farm the sea and soon the tide turned, the water deepened, and we all scurried back to the beach to await the next ebb tide.

Constance Salerno Narro

5356 Mortons Ford Way
Haymarket, Virginia 20169
703-425-0510
art@ngti.com

Flower Burst

watercolor, 20 x 29

Art has been an important part of my life from childhood. I have studied and practiced in a number of media, sketching in charcoal/pastels, painting in oils/watercolors, and making ceramics and pottery. After receiving my BA and MA, I taught high school art appreciation for seven years. However, it wasn't until our family moved to Northern Virginia in 1972 that watercolors became my primary focus and passion. This medium has given me the best opportunity to engage in painting interesting and challenging subjects, especially flowers and people. Flower species are vast; many are unique and amenable to arrangements that are beautiful, with vibrant colors and textures. They are an inexhaustible subject with vast venues for exploiting their beauty. *Flower Burst* is just that — a burst. There is no sharp focal point; attention is drawn to all the flowers guided by the green in the background. I found this harder to do than a traditional floral painting. I hope that viewers, after their initial impressions, will scan the arrangement to enjoy the specific aspects that spark their attention.

Chica Brunsvold

3510 Wentworth Drive
Falls Church, Virginia 22044
703-256-1985
chicabrunsvold@gmail.com
chicabrunsvold.com

For the past 20 years, I have begun my paintings in a strictly non-objective manner, which makes painting an adventure from the very first splash of color. I use broad movements, putting on color, wiping it off, and adding textures by using anything that is handy. Foam brushes and rollers, scraping tools, stamps that I carve, spray bottles, and facial tissues for wiping are all useful. This painting was done on Yupo, which allows for endless possibilities, as paint sits on top of the surface and can easily be removed and reapplied. I constantly study my painting for images that I can make visible to others. I take off my glasses and view the painting from all angles, in the mirror, and often in semi-darkness. Sometimes I see flowers, but more often animal shapes – Zooillogicals®. What fun! After I discover images, I put my glasses back on and set to work revising and refining. It can go on and on, but I like that. Painting this way is great fun for me and guarantees that my work is unique.

Birdbath

watercolor, 21 x 27

Leigh Culver

202-232-0788
leigh.culver@gmail.com

This subject depicts the white sand island of South Plaza on the Galapagos. When I was there, the undergrowth was in its seasonal splendor of reds and golds. I used the direct approach to painting – getting it down *au premier coup* – and mixed the colors directly on the hot press paper. Incorporating splatters, I wanted this to celebrate both nature and paint.

Galapagos Autumn

watercolor, 9 x 12

Nancy Brown

2 Bowen Mill Road
Baltimore, Maryland 21212
nancywbrown@aol.com
nancybrownart.com

Uptown is the result of several visits to New York City. I love to walk through the various neighborhoods looking for unusual architecture and light. Riding the subway frequently inspired me to paint this subject with people rushing in all directions. The cabs are everywhere and accent the streets with color. An accurate drawing provides a foundation for my painting. I mask out my lightest areas first and use a pouring technique to lay in the first layer of paint. To do this, I place red and blue in two separate cups and dilute them with water, then pour the colors onto the paper allowing them to mix. I then mask the mid-tone values and pour on another layer of paint. To pull the painting together, I use a brush to add the details and accent colors. To create the colors of the street, I use a sponge to move the paint in a downward motion.

Uptown
watercolor, 25 x 19

Rachel B. Collins

Torpedo Factory Art Center Studio 342
105 North Union Street
Alexandria, Virginia 22314
703-838-9695
rbcollins@yahoo.com
rachelcollinsart.com

This painting is part of an ongoing series of music-themed paintings that I have been developing over the past few years as a way of combining two great loves: making art and making music. I often focus on the individual beauty of the instruments taken as models; in this case, the repetitive shapes of the keys and tone holes of B-flat clarinets and the silhouettes of the edges of the instruments. Painting in transparent watercolor is not unlike playing music: once a sound is released, the musician cannot call it back, just as the painter can never completely undo a color laid down on the surface of the paper. I build most of my paintings in a series of layers, thereby making chords of color, sometimes in dense clusters, sometimes in the softest translucence. I find that often the key to successful glazing and layering of color is the removal of some of the external sizing on the 300 lb. paper on which I usually work.

Clarinets on Fire!
watercolor, 28 x 21

Catherine Hillis

P. O. Box 41
Round Hill, Virginia 20142
703-431-6877
info@catherinehillis.com
catherinehillis.com
catherinehillispaints.blogspot.com

I live in Round Hill, Virginia, in the foothills of the Blue Ridge mountains, along a twisting gravel road that was a major thoroughfare west during the 18th century. All around me is the scenery I love: the tumbledown barns, grazing sheep, stone walls, verdant pastures and – my own personal mountain.

I love to play with light patterns and often with a playful twist. While I enjoy painting the beautiful rural landscape around me, *en plein air*, I'm just as interested in capturing the urban scene, with its intoxicating energy, architecture, crowds of figures and reflections.

I have a passion for painting and I paint every day in my north light studio when I'm not participating in *plein air* and national competitions, or teaching. I invite you to observe the complexity of city and country, suburban and urban, and the yin and yang of life, seeing color in a new way.

From Giotto's Bell Tower
watercolor, 26 x 20

176

PVW Members 2013

Olene Albertson BWS

Marge Alderson

Martha Allen

Mary Allen

Mary Cannell Andrews

Sarah Andrews

Terry Anstrom VWS

Judy Antico BWS, VWS

Neyla Arnas

Patria E. Baranski

Helen Dilley Barsalou WHS, VWS, BWS

Brenda C. Barthell VWS

Marie Baumann

Karen H. Beach

Connie Boland BWS, MPSGS

Carol Bouville BWS

Gwendolyn C. Bragg NWS, VWS, BWS

Toni Bragg

Nancy Brown BWS, DWS

Chica Brunsvold AWS, NWS, NWWS

Mary Ruth Buchness

Deborah Brisker Burk

Jan H. Burns

Heather Mackay Butler

Betty Calabria

Nellie Chao

Gina P. Clapp

Jim Cobren

Kathryn Cochrane

Deb Cohan BWS

Elizabeth Collard BWS

Rachel B. Collins NWS, TWSA, WHS

Shelby Conley

Deborah Conn BWS, VWS

Jane McElvany Coonce

Lassie L. Corbett VWS

Eleanor Cox SW, BWS, VWS

Johanna (Joan) L. Crane

Francesca Creo

Leigh Culver

Betsy LeBleu Curry VWS

Roberta Day VWS

Mak Dehejia

Ellen F. Delaney

Tricia DeWeese BWS

Jacquelyn J. Dinora BWS

Prudence Waugh Donovan VWS

William Doying

Peggy-Ann K. Duke

Bernice B. Duvall BWS, PWS

Muriel Ebitz BWS

Lella Lee Edwards VWS

Mary Eggers BWS, ISAP

Carol Debolt Eikenbery

Deborah Marshall Elliott VWS

Chris Engnoth

Ruth Ensley

Marcia Gladsky Esquibel

Marilyn Feldman

Donna Finnegan

Laura Loree Fisher

Natalie R. Fleming BWS, MOWS

Janet J. Ford VWS

Yolanda Frederikse

Kay Fuller BWS

Leigh Alison Fulton

Betty Ganley BWS, VWS

Cathleen F. Gardner

Carolyn Grossé Gawarecki NWS, WHS, VWS

Sarah Gerould

Lieta Gerson

Jean K. Gill, AWS, NWS

David Gillenwater

Lisa Gillispie BWS

Patricia C. Givens

Jane Gott

Judith Gray

Linda Griffin

Michelle Guilmain

Debra Grayer Halprin BWS, PWCS

Margitta Hanff VWS

Anne Hanna BWS, DWS

Jack Harding BWS

Virginia Hayward

Rob Henry

Lorrie Herman

Susan Herron NWS

Christine A. Heyse BWS

Vera Heywood

Catherine Hillis SW, PWS, WCWS

Kathryn Grill Hoeppel BWS, PWS

Elaine S. Hoffman BWS

Margaret Huddy AWS, NWS, WHS

Ardythe Jolliff WHS, SW, PWCS

Jane S. Jordan

Alice Kale BWS, VWS

LeAnn Kalita BWS

Monna Kauppinen

Graciela Congote Keane

Dell Keathley BWS

Anne Noble Kehr BWS

Brenda Will Kidera

Joan Kirk

Linda H. Kirvan

Yolanda Koh BWS

Stephanie Kozemchak

Teresa Kramer

Margaret Graham Kranking AWS, NWS

Charlotte Landis

Christine Lashley BWS

Roslyn Perluck Latto

Marni M. Lawson PWS, BWS, VWS

Amanda Lee VWS

Pat Leibowitz BWS

Laura Lemley

Bonita Lestina

Trudy Levy

Cindi Lewis

Liang Wei

Barry D. Lindley BWS

Roberta P. Lintner

Gloria Logan

Joan Lok BWS

Pauline Davis Lorfano VWS, BWS, ISMP

Ruth E. Lotz BWS

Meg MacKenzie VWS, BWS

Linda E. Maldonado

Barbara J. Maloney

Marni Maree

Yoshimi S. Matsukata BWS

Judelle McArdle

Emilie D. McBride

Loy McGaughy

Marilyn Milici VWS

Harris C. Miller

Miyoko Mizuno

Jamaliah Morais

Sydney Morgan BWS

Elinor Morley

Sue Moses BWS

Connie Salerno Narro

Anthony (Tony) Neville

Kate Niner

Karen Norman BWS

Rosemary Nothwanger BWS, VWS, GWS

Elaine Nunnally VWS, BWS, MOWS

Virginia C. O'Rourke

Traci Oberle

Sally H. Olson

Margaret Mather Pearson (MAGZ)

Fae Penland

Mary Phelan

Lynda D. Pitman

Patricia N. Porter

Jill E. Poyerd NWS, PWS

Regina E. Price

JoAnne Ramsey BWS

Michele Rea, NWS

Therese 'Terri' Rea

Elise Ritter

Liz Roberts NWS, VWS

Betzi Robinson

Grace Rooney

Patrick Roth

Sheldon Ruben

Susan J. Rubenstein

Colleen M. Sabo AAA, CLWAC, BWS

Frances Salo

Jane B. Salomon

Rebecca Salzinger

Ginger Sanaie

Jacqueline Saunders VWS

Concetta C. Scott BWS, PWCS, VWS

Karin Sebolka

Florence Setzer VWS

Marie Kaneko Shaughnessy VWS

Dale Sheldon BWS, DWS

Linda J. Sherman BWS, TWS

Mary Lou Shields

Millie S. Shott

Anna M. Shuman

Jane Cordes Simanis

Carol Richardson Simmons

Vita M. Sims

Marilyn Skaggs

Julie Smith BWS

Jung Lea Smith

Ruth Soldz

Frank H. Spink VWS

Margy Stancill

Carroll M. Stone

Donna Sturm BWS, VWS

Peter Suchman

Margaret M. Suddeth BWS, VWS

Barbara Sullivan

Katherine Sullivan BWS, VWS

Jane S. Thomas

Amy Thompson

Gretchen Thompson

Ruth G. Thomson

Irene Tsai

Karen Ceolla Tylec NAWA, BWS

Jeanne Thornhill Ulrich

Peter B. Ulrich BWS

Rosa Vera BWS

Carol Vorosmarti

Peggy Talbot Wagner

Nancy Walnes VWS

Anne Beach Was

Alice Webb BWS, PWS, LWS

Elaine Weiner-Reed

Judy Wengrovitz SW, VWS, BWS

Harriet Westfall BWS, VWS

Tammy Wiedenhaefer BWS

Madeline Wikler BWS

Marjean Willett BWS, PWCS

Dana Winslow

Connie Ward Woolard BWS, PWCS

Carolyn Marshall Wright

Deborah Pool Wurzel BWS

SIGNATURE MEMBERSHIPS

AAA Allied Artists of America

AWS American Watercolor Society

BWS Baltimore Watercolor Society

CLWAC Catharine Lorillard Wolfe Art Club

DWS Delaware Watercolor Society

GWS Georgia Watercolor Society

ISAP International Society of Acrylic Painters

ISMP International Society of Marine Painters

LWS Louisiana Watercolor Society

MOWS Missouri Watercolor Society

MPSGS Miniature Painters, Sculptors and Gravers Society

NAWA National Association of Women Artists

NWS National Watercolor Society

NWWS Northwest Watercolor Society

PWCS Philadelphia Watercolor Society

PWS Pennsylvania Watercolor Society

SW Southern Watercolor Society

TWS Texas Watercolor Society

TWSA Transparent Watercolor Society of America

VWS Virginia Watercolor Society

WCWS Western Colorado Watercolor Society

WHS Watercolor USA Honor Society

In Memoriam

Carl Barnes

Kathleen Bishop

Joel Bitman BWS

Shirley Bounds VWS

Puff Brooks

Mary Duer Brown SW

Jacqueline De Moss BWS

Wendy Dellett

Liz Donovan NWS, BWS

Joan Edlow PWS, PWCS, BWS

Ranson Ludwig Eng

Marlin Edward Fenical

Helen Garretson AWS, NWS, BWS

Valerie Gulick

Ann Eldredge Hall

Kenton D. Hamaker

Carol Hammett VWS

Arthur F. Harless

Zetta Jones VWS

Ted MacKechnie VWS, past president PVW

C. Christine Maxwell BWS

B. Allen Mays

Roddy McLean

Don Mundt

Jeannette Niska

Marion Ott

Bethea Scott Owen VWS

Sid Platt BWS

Barbara Bettis Quackenbush

Cornelia Raring VWS

Helen Reichardt VWS

Carole Coy Richardson

Coy Roy, VWS

Jill Schlanser

Jacqueline Monroe Schwarz

Irene Snelling Smyth VWS

Evelyn Spindler

Gail Stafford

Mary Anne Tennant

Shirley Wiggin VWS

Carolyn Zakaski

Index of Artists Represented in the Book